THE
ART NOUVEAU
STYLE

THE ART NOUVEAU STYLE

IN JEWELRY, METALWORK, GLASS, CERAMICS, TEXTILES, ARCHITECTURE AND FURNITURE

EDITED BY

ROBERTA WADDELL

DOVER PUBLICATIONS, INC.
NEW YORK

Published in Canada by General Publishing Company, Ltd., 30 Lesmill
Road, Don Mills, Toronto, Ontario.
Published in the United Kingdom by Constable and Company, Ltd.,
10 Orange Street, London WC2H 7EG.

The Art Nouveau Style is a new work, first published by Dover Publications, Inc., in 1977. The illustrations are reproduced from *Art et
Décoration: Revue Mensuelle d'Art Moderne*, Librairie Centrale des
Beaux-Arts, Paris, 1897–1911. They were selected by Roberta Waddell,
who also prepared the Introduction, captions and Biographical Sketches.

International Standard Book Number: 0–486–23515–7
Library of Congress Catalog Card Number: 77–80034

Manufactured in the United States of America
Dover Publications, Inc.
180 Varick Street
New York, N.Y. 10014

CONTENTS

INTRODUCTION

At the end of the nineteenth century, European newsstands and bookstores were flooded with new magazines and journals dealing with the applied arts—approximately one hundred appeared between 1890 and 1900. The plates presented in this book are selected from one of these periodicals, the Paris journal *Art et Décoration*. The designs reveal the international scope of enthusiasm for the decorative arts—from jewelry to table settings and furniture—all sharing an ornamental vocabulary that crossed national borders.

"Art Nouveau" is the name popularly associated today with this international style which manifested itself most consistently in the applied arts, less so in painting, sculpture, and architecture. During the 1890's and the early years of the twentieth century, the movement we now designate as Art Nouveau was identified by a variety of names in different countries. In Germany these labels included the descriptive "Schörkelstil" (flourish style) and "Bandwurmstil" (tapeworm style), though "Jugendstil" (after the Munich journal *Jugend*) gained the widest acceptance. The epithets "Paling Stijl" (eel style) and "Style Nouille" (noodle style) were popular in Belgium. In Italy "Stile Inglese" (English style) and "Stile Liberty" (after the shop Liberty of London) paid homage to the English role in encouraging the decorative-arts movement. The French in turn acknowledged the British contributions with the label "Modern Style" (a name also used in Belgium), while Edmond de Goncourt somewhat disparagingly named the movement "Yachting Style" when the Belgian artist-craftsman Henry van de Velde had his first exhibition in Paris.

Samuel Bing, a native of Hamburg living in Paris, first introduced the expression "Art Nouveau." In 1885 Bing opened a shop at 22 rue de Provence which specialized in Japanese art. In December, 1895, Bing reorganized his business to promote the current revival of interest in the decorative arts. For his opening exhibition Bing commissioned Bonnard, Grasset, Ibels, Roussel, Sérusier, Toulouse-Lautrec, Ranson, Vallotton, and Vuillard to provide designs for stained glass which would be executed by Louis Comfort Tiffany. There were also sculptures by Rodin and paintings by Carrière, Denis, Khnopff, and the painters who had contributed the stained-glass designs. Emile Gallé and Tiffany exhibited glass while Lalique displayed jewelry. There were posters by the English illustrator Aubrey Beardsley, by Will H. Bradley, an American, and by Charles Rennie Mackintosh, a Scot. Reigning over this international display of arts and crafts was the shop's sign, described by Arsène Alexandre, editor of the *Revue des Art Décoratifs*, as "two enormous sun aureoles with their round discs, violently exaggerated, with neither taste nor style . . . [accompanied by] these two words in their delightful modesty: *art nouveau*."

Although the style was seen as "new," an interest in the applied arts had been well established during the second half of the nineteenth century. The Great Exhibition of 1851 had pointed out the sorry state of household design; in both England and on the Continent the crisis in the decorative arts was met by official action.

Great Britain quickly rallied to educate the next generation of artist-craftsmen. In 1852 the government established the Department of Practical Art (later renamed the Department of Science and Art), and in 1853 the Victoria and Albert Museum was founded to serve as a teaching institution as well as a museum. Individual Englishmen encouraged the study of good design. Ruskin and the

Pre-Raphaelites taught at the Workingman's Guild which was created in 1854. In 1882 Arthur Mackmurdo and Selwyn Image founded the Century Guild; this association and The Art Workers Guild (established in 1884) participated in the Arts and Crafts Exhibition Society's shows (founded in 1888), where the public was introduced to models of fine craftsmanship.

The leading exponent of the Arts and Crafts Movement in England was William Morris who, through his personal example and the work of those who designed for Morris & Co., encouraged interest in the decorative arts in England, on the Continent, and in the United States. Champion of an idealized Middle Ages and a socialist, Morris believed that handicrafts could bring joy to the maker as well as to the consumer. He asserted that every man had the right to live among beautifully designed and crafted objects. "I don't want art for a few, any more than education for a few, or freedom for a few. . . . What business have we with art at all unless all can share it."

Whereas Morris saw the revival of crafts as part of the solution for the social ills of nineteenth-century Britain, some of his fellow Englishmen, members of the Aesthetic Movement (including James McNeill Whistler and Oscar Wilde), saw the cultivation of the decorative arts as an end in itself. For these "Decadents," as they were called, the appreciation of art for art's sake was a suitable goal in life. Though their objectives differed, they shared with the members of the Arts and Crafts Movement a common appreciation for the applied arts, from the beautifully bound book to the well-designed piece of furniture.

In France the government similarly encouraged a revival of the decorative arts. The Société du Progrès de l'Art Industriel, established in 1858, sponsored an exhibition of applied art in 1861 and another in 1863, the year in which the Union Centrale des Beaux-Arts Appliqués à l'Industrie was founded, partly in response to the great strides made by English designers and craftsmen. In 1882 the Union Centrale des Beaux-Arts merged with the Société du Musée des Arts Décoratifs (established in 1877) to form the Union Centrale des Arts Décoratifs with its publication *Revue des Arts Décoratifs*.

Those interested in art education, crafts societies, exhibitions of the decorative arts, and the philosophy of "art for art's sake" believed in the equality of all the arts. For example, the Century Guild had been founded "to render all branches of art the sphere no longer of the tradesman, but of the artist. It would restore building, decoration, glass-painting, pottery, wood-carving, and metal to their right place beside painting and sculpture." For William Morris, the artist himself had to be a man of many talents. "If a chap can't compose an epic poem while he's weaving a tapestry, he had better shut up, he'll never do any good at all." Beginning in the second half of the century, there were a number of versatile artists. Morris wrote, painted, and worked at a number of crafts; Dante Gabriel Rossetti was poet and painter. Christopher Dresser, Walter Crane, and Owen Jones were theoreticians as well as designers; Crane was also a respected painter. Later, in the 1890's, Obrist, Endell, Gallé, Guimard, and van de Velde wrote on art and at the same time excelled as craftsmen-designers.

In the 1880's and 1890's many of those who devoted themselves to the crafts hoped to break with the historicism which had dominated earlier nineteenth-century applied art. They rejected the study of past styles and the wholesale application of ornament from historical models to contemporary objects. As the name "Art Nouveau" implies, they wished to create a new art, heralding the arrival of the new century. An artist, however, cannot completely divorce himself from the past, and the Art Nouveau craftsman also drew upon his art heritage.

The study of nature had preoccupied the nineteenth-century artist. Owen Jones and Christopher Dresser had warned in various treatises that the artist-craftsman should not copy, but rather should simplify nature and derive rules of design from it. The turn-of-the-century craftsmen followed this advice and, like Eugène Grasset and Emile Gallé (both botany students), explored the decorative qualities and symbolic energy present in organic forms.

The study of Japanese art assisted the Art Nouveau artist in his efforts to simplify nature. Throughout the century artists and designers had been fascinated by foreign art, especially painting and crafts from Persia, India, and Turkey. The opening of Japan to the West in 1853 began the flood of Japanese art to England and the Continent and added one more exotic style to the nineteenth-century repertoire. To the sensitive craftsman this new material offered important artistic lessons. Japanese color woodblock prints were especially instructive. The Japanese artist-craftsman simplified and made nature and the human form decorative through flat, often asymmetrical arrangements of color and pattern linked by bold, curving outlines.

When the late nineteenth-century craftsman turned to other exotic cultures for inspiration, he selected those elements which were compatible with his interest in two-dimensional, relatively abstract, often curvilinear design. He studied the decorative batik textiles introduced from Java by Dutch importers. He learned another ornamental vocabulary from the study of Egyptian art, popular interest in which began in the 1880's and continued through the end of the century. He studied Celtic art, much publicized by recent historical research and archaeological discoveries. The "entrelac" design, the dragon, and the two-dimensional coils found in Irish book illustration and goldsmith work were especially popular in England, Ireland, Scotland, and Scandinavia.

Earlier European and English art also offered sources of decorative ornament. In England the work of William Blake was of particular interest to members of the Century Guild and to Rossetti, who collected, studied, and wrote about his illustrated books. Blake's evocative, emotional, curvilinear drawings and engravings, which had struck a responsive note in the Pre-Raphaelites, continued to fascinate artists for the rest of the century. On the Continent in the 1880's and 1890's the Rococo Revival, and to a lesser extent the Baroque Revival, reintroduced plastic, asymmetrical, curvilinear ornament to the applied arts and architecture. Some craftsmen were influenced by the sinuous decoration found in Gothic architecture, which was already championed by William Morris, A. W. N. Pugin, John Ruskin, and Viollet-le-Duc.

These various historical and foreign sources set the stage for the appearance of the mature Art Nouveau which blossomed first in France and Belgium in the early 1890's, then in Scotland, and later in Germany and Austria. In England, in spite of the fascination with Japanese art and the interest in nature, the works of the Aesthetic Movement and the Arts and Crafts Movement manifested only infrequently the fully developed Art Nouveau style.

Though difficult to define, Art Nouveau—whether found in a Gallé vase, a Horta light fixture, a van de Velde buckle, a Lalique necklace, or a Hoffmann interior—is a style of surface ornament dominated by pervasive curvilinear rhythms. During a period when artists, writers, and musicians wished to synthesize all the arts, these serpentine patterns not only encompassed and unified the Art Nouveau object, but also fused it with its surroundings which shared and echoed these decorative rhythms. Art Nouveau is seen at its best in interior design where the artist-craftsman sought to interrelate accessories, furniture, and the architectural treatment of walls and ceiling.

The linear and surface rhythms which dominate the object and bring it into a relationship with its environment are generally curvilinear and asymmetrical, though each country had a special hallmark, its own decorative vocabulary. A brief discussion of different national stylistic characteristics, with reference to the work of a few individual craftsmen, can give an idea of the variety of decorative forms possible within the Art Nouveau style.

In France Art Nouveau art and architecture can be identified by an undulating, graceful, sometimes whiplash line which suggests the influence of the late Gothic and Rococo periods. Ornament from the Nancy school, exemplified by the glass and furniture designs of Emile Gallé, is quite naturalistic, whereas Parisian Art Nouveau, represented by the work of de Feure and Gaillard, is more austere and abstract.

Art Nouveau ornament in Belgium is often plastic, forceful, and abstract. The decorative vocabulary assumes a variety of forms, from the dynamic decoration found in the interior of a house by Victor Horta and the powerful, ponderous, three-dimensional structural furniture of Henry van de Velde, to the light, constructive juxtapositions of curves and right angles in household designs by Gustave Serrurier-Bovy, inspired by the English Arts and Crafts Movement.

In Scottish Art Nouveau the rhythms of line are quite different from the French whiplash and the Belgian plastic curves. The elegant, attenuated curves, the refined, two-dimensional, linear surface ornament found in the work of "The Four" (Charles Rennie Mackintosh, Herbert MacNair, Margaret and Frances Macdonald) typify Scottish Art Nouveau, with its center at the Glasgow School of Art.

Fully developed Art Nouveau in Germany reflects both the influence of Belgian artists (particularly of Henry van de Velde, who exhibited and taught there) and of the more austere, constructive designs popularized by the English Arts and Crafts Movement. A line that thickens at the point of the curve is a hallmark of both naturalistic and abstract German Art Nouveau ornament. This device is found everywhere—in furniture designs, in vignettes for books, even in type faces.

Art Nouveau came late to Austria. By the turn of the century the organic rhythms of ornament are stilled to a near-classical calm and are contained within rectilinear shapes, quite similar to and possibly influenced by designs from the Glasgow School of Art. A certain decorative vocabulary employing a symmetrical tree motif and the juxtaposition of the square and the circle was typical of this Austrian school, as evident in the work of Josef Hoffmann and Joseph Olbrich.

The various styles of Art Nouveau ornament were considered to be more than simple surface decoration and were imbued with significant inner meaning. Oscar Wilde suggested this in *The Picture of Dorian Gray:* "All art is at once surface and symbol." Just as the Symbolists had rejected realism in poetry for the evocation of a reality through sound and rhythm, the Art Nouveau artist-craftsman sought deeper significance through decorative form. For Emile Gallé and others this could mean a quotation from Maeterlinck inscribed verbatim on a vase or a table. For still others the method was more subtle. Influenced by Seurat and the theories of Charles Henry, many late nineteenth-century painters and decorators believed that by careful choice of color and line, the artist could suggest hidden meanings and evoke an emotional reaction in the beholder.

For the Art Nouveau artist, line was the most expressive way to elicit these subtle feelings. As early as 1892 Walter Crane lectured in England: "Hence LINE is all-important. Let the designer, therefore, in the adaptation of this art, lean upon the staff of *line*—line determinative, line emphatic, line delicate, line expressive, line controlling, and uniting." After the turn of the century Eugène Grasset wrote, "Every curve gives the idea of movement and life . . . the trace of the curve should be full, rounded, firm, and harmonious like a stalk full of young sap." Henry van de Velde succinctly stated his view: "*Linie is eine Kraft*" (line is a force).

In Art Nouveau ornament, line—whether "expressive" or "controlling"—is organic and full of life, for nature was the primary theme for the artist-craftsman. New, unfamiliar, and often unlikely subjects were popular: sea life, including fish, the octopus, jelly fish, and seaweed. Snakes, dragonflies, and bats decorated a variety of applied arts. The germinating bud and the wandering tendril were readily adapted to the curvilinear rhythms favored by the period. The human figure was apt to appear as a woman with long, flowing tresses. Often emaciated and childlike, she was both threatening and erotic.

If the public was at first bewildered by the choice of subject matter and the treatment of the decorative arts at the turn of the century, the plethora of magazines and numerous exhibitions quickly familiarized the viewers and assured the acceptance of the new style, even its ultimate fashionableness. The English took the lead in publicizing the crafts movement in the 1880's, first with the Century Guild's magazine *Hobby Horse* and then, slightly later, with *The Dial.* In 1893 *The Studio* began publication (the American edition appeared in 1897), introducing its readers to new developments in decorative art reproducing the work of leading British and Continental illustrators and craftsmen. Abroad, *Pan* (Berlin, 1895–1900) became the first periodical on the Continent to promote Art Nouveau in a richly decorated and illustrated journal of art and literature. *Jugend* (1896–1914), a lighter, witty journal, was published in Munich and quickly became identified with the new art. After founding *Pan*, Meier-Graefe went on to encourage the applied arts in *Dekorative Kunst* (1897–1929), and in the following year he published a French counterpart, *L'Art Décoratif*. In 1897 *Art et Décoration*, the journal from which the pictures in this book have been selected, imitated the layout of *The Studio*. Like that English journal, it aimed its articles at a lay audience. In this same year in Darmstadt, Alexander Koch, who already published *Inner-Dekoration* (1890–1944), began *Deutsche Kunst und Dekoration* (1897–1934). Other German periodicals which fostered Art Nouveau include *Kunst und Handwerk* (Munich, 1898–1932) and *Modern Stil* (Stuttgart, 1899–1905). As the focus of Art Nouveau shifted to Vienna, the style was promoted in *Der Architekt* (1895–1922) and in the monthly magazine of the Museum of Art and Industry, *Kunst und Kunsthandwerk* (1898–1921). One of the most beautiful of the Art Nouveau journals rivaling *Pan* was *Ver Sacrum* (1898–1903), the periodical of the Vienna Secession, which included graphic art and illustration along with literature.

These journals reported on the numerous exhibitions of applied arts which thrived in every country. In England the Arts and Crafts Exhibition Society held shows in 1888, 1889, 1890, 1893, and 1896. Belgium, responsive to both English and Continental art movements, had since 1884 displayed avant-garde art under the auspices of "Les XX." In 1892 "Les XX" showed decorative arts for the first time, including stained glass, embroidery, ceramics, and illustrated books along with painting and sculpture. By 1894, when the association's name was changed to La Libre Esthétique, the equality of all the arts was accepted. Included in the 1894 show were illustrations by Beardsley and Toorop, silver by Ashbee, and a studio interior by Serrurier-Bovy. William Morris was represented by wallpapers, fabrics, and Kelmscott Press books. Designs from the Glasgow School of Art were first displayed on the Continent at an exhibition in Liège in 1895, along with the work of other British craftsmen-artists, including Burne Jones, Ashbee, Crane, and Morris.

Germany first presented applied arts at the Glaspalast Exhibition in 1897, introducing the work of Eckmann, Endell, Obrist, and Riemerschmid. In this same year a major show in Dresden included whole sections of Samuel Bing's shop, L'Art Nouveau, and the work of Henry van de Velde. The first exhibition of decorative art in Austria, which took place in 1898, presented the work of Hoffmann and Obrist; the following year their work appeared side by side with that of van de Velde and Pankok.

In France applied art was shown with wall paintings at the 1891 Salon de Champs de Mars. Individual artists also sponsored craft exhibitions. In 1895 a new group of five artist-craftsmen ("Les Cinq"—Alexander Charpentier, Jean Dampt, Félix Aubert, Tony Selmersheim, and Etienne Moreau-Nélaton) held a show of their work. In 1896, as "Les Six," they included the work of Charles Plumet, and in 1897 as "L'Art dans Tout," they also presented crafts by Henri Nocq. When Samuel Bing opened the doors of L'Art Nouveau in 1895 he announced his support of the decorative arts. Through his store he encouraged and patronized a group of young artist-craftsmen, including Georges de Feure, Eugène Gaillard, and Edward Colonna.

These Bing associates were among the leading lights of the Paris World's Fair of 1900. At what was essentially a celebration of the French decorative-arts movement, the French were unrivalled, but at the Turin Exhibition in 1902 a number of other countries displayed their achievements in the applied arts. From England came Voysey and Ashbee; from Scotland, "The Four"; from Belgium, Victor Horta, van de Velde, Serrurier-Bovy; from Austria, Hoffmann; and from Germany, Behrens, Pankok, and Koepping. The French did not even exhibit at the 1905 exhibition at Liège.

By 1905 it was clear that the heyday of Art Nouveau was over. French Art Nouveau gave way to a more traditional style reminiscent of Louis XV and XVI. In Germany, Scotland, and Austria decoration was gradually abandoned and that which remained was geometric. The organic, vital line was stilled. By 1910 the style lived on only in commercial designs.

Although short-lived, Art Nouveau made a lasting contribution to the decorative arts. The artist-craftsmen raised the status of the applied arts to rival the position of the so-called fine arts. Their concern for fine craftsmanship counteracted the shoddy workmanship which had appalled nineteenth-century critics. The attention with which these craftsmen created harmonious and unified interiors was a lesson not lost by twentieth-century designers. Perhaps most important, the Art Nouveau craftsmen, by breaking away from the historicism of their predecessors, paved the way for new developments in art and architecture—the "modern movement," where "organic" no longer referred to a style of decoration, but implied that form be determined by function. When the Art Nouveau craftsmen created a new vocabulary of ornament, they freed their artistic descendants from historical models, and gave them the right to dispense with ornament altogether.

ROBERTA WADDELL

New York
April, 1977

JEWELRY

1. Ornament, Lucien Gaillard.

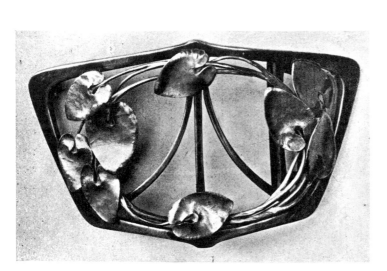

2

3

4

2 & 3. *Buckle and pendant, Paul-Emile Brandt.*   4. *Hairpins, Lucien Gaillard.*

5

6

7

8

5. *Comb, Henri Vever.*   6 & 7. *Brooch and jewelry case, Eugène Feuillâtre.*   8. *Pendant, Paul-Emile Brandt.*

10

11

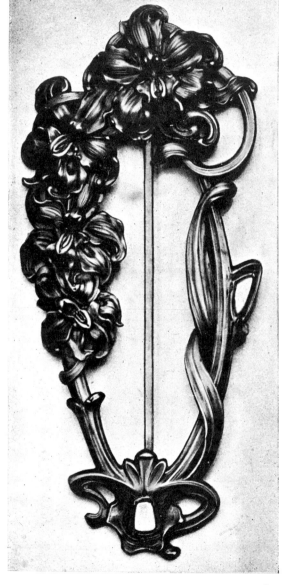

9

12

9. Buckle, G. Laffitte.   10 & 11. Pendants, Georges Fouquet.   12. Comb, René Lalique.

13

14

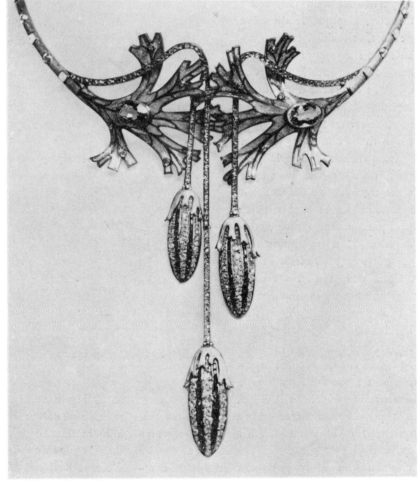

16

15

13 & 15. Pendants, Georges Fouquet.   14. Bracelet, Edward Colonna.   16. Hatpin, Paul-Emile Brandt.

17

18

20   19

17. *Brooch, Eugène Feuillâtre.*   18. *Brooch, Philippe Wolfers.*   19.   *Brooch, René Lalique.*
20. *Pendant, Lucien Gaillard.*

21

22

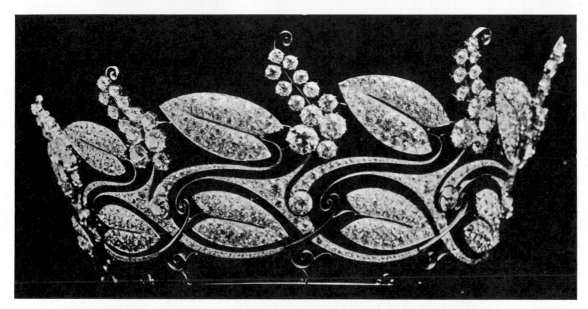

23

24

*21. Pendant, Maison Vever.   22. Pendants, Peter Wyler Davidson.   23. Tiara, Frédéric Boucheron.
24. Clasp, Agnes Bankier Harvey.*

25

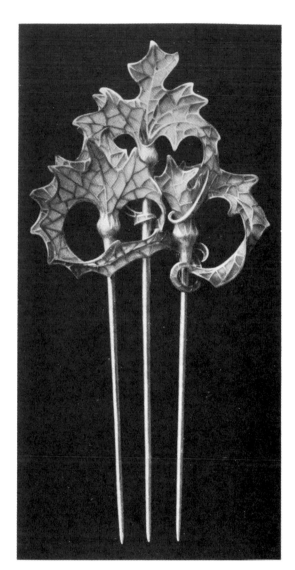

27

26

28

25. *Brooch, Henri Vever, design by Eugène Grasset.*   26. *Hairpin, Maison Vever.*   27. *Comb, Lucien Gaillard.*
28. *Bracelet, René Lalique.*

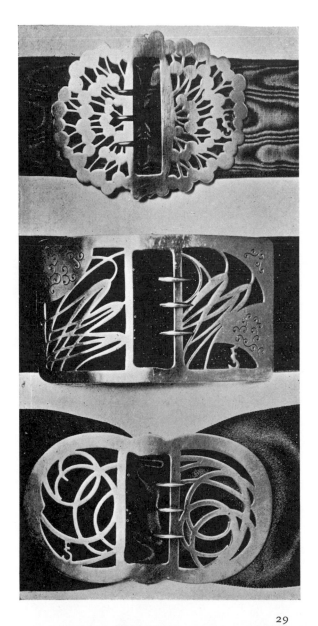

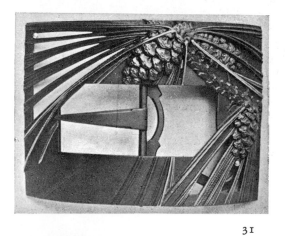

29

30

31

32

29. *Buckles, Paul Frank Scheidecker.* 30. *Money box, Edmond Henri Becker.* 31. *Buckle, Lucien Gaillard.*
32. *Jewelry box, Mlle de Félice.*

33

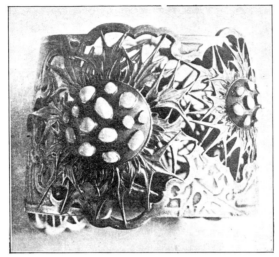

34

35

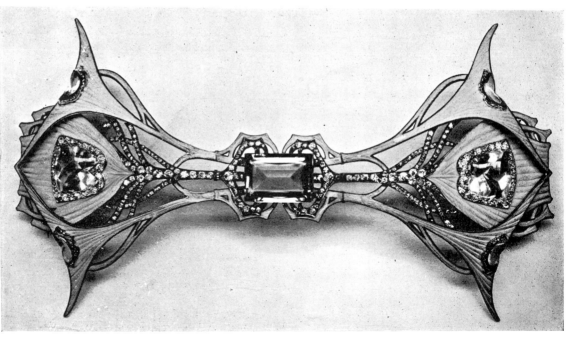

36

33 & 34. Hatpin and bracelet, René Lalique.   35 & 36. Pendant and brooch, Lucien Gaillard.

37

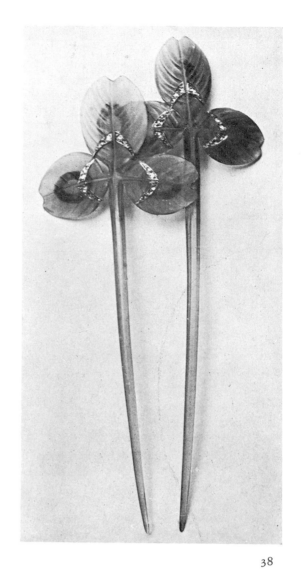

38

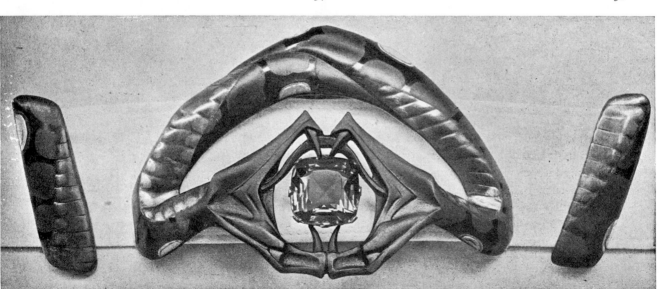

39

37. *Jewelry box, Mme Martin Sabon.*   38. *Hairpin, Paul Liénard.*   39. *Buckle, Lucien Gaillard.*

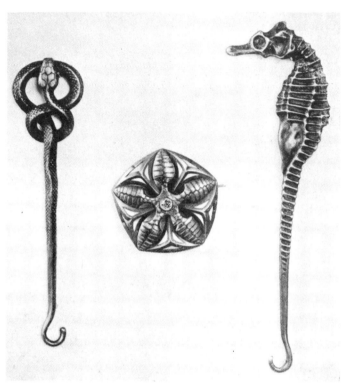

40

41

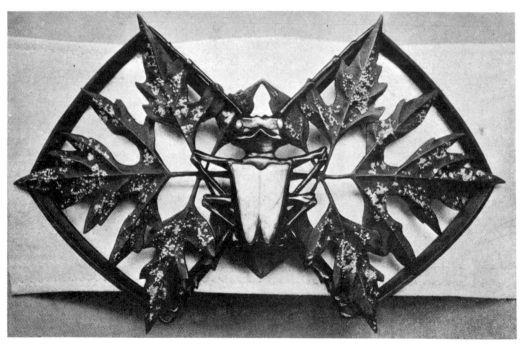

42

40. *Shoe buttons and brooch, L. Gardey.*   41. *Buckle, Henri Vever, design by Eugène Grasset.*
42. *Buckle, Lucien Gaillard.*

43

44

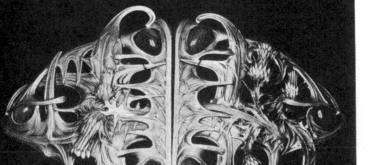

45

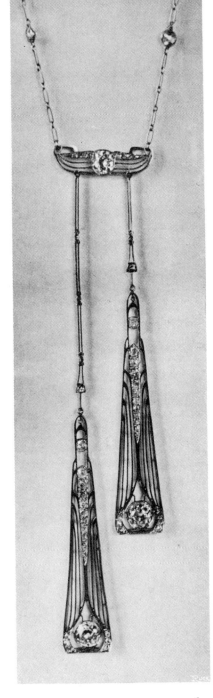

46

43. *Pendant, Philippe Wolfers.*　44. *Buckle, Lucien Gaillard.*　45. *Buckle, Laffitte and Wasley.*
46. *Pendant, Maurice Dufrène.*

47

48

49

47. *Pendant, Maison Vever.*   48. *Brooch, René Lalique.*   49. *Silver jewelry box, Richard Llewelyn Benson Rathbone.*

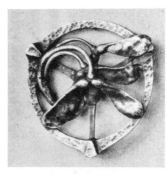

50

51

52

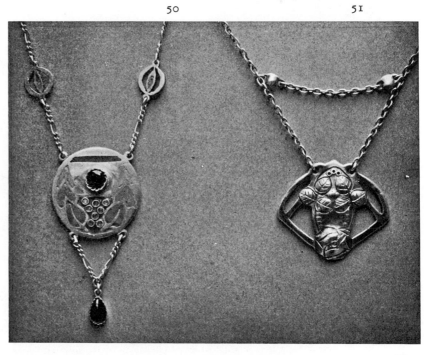

53

50. *Clasp, Henri Husson.*   51. *Buckle, Paul-Emile Brandt.*   52. *Buckle, Maison Vever, design by Eugène Grasset.*
53. *Pendants, Isabel Spence.*

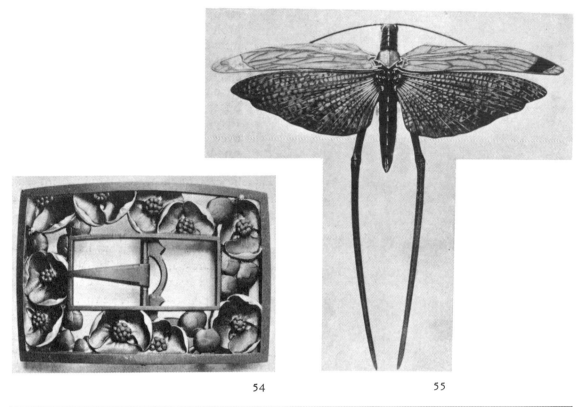

54   55

56

54 & 55. Buckle and hairpin, Lucien Gaillard.   56. Jewelry box, Victor Prouvé.

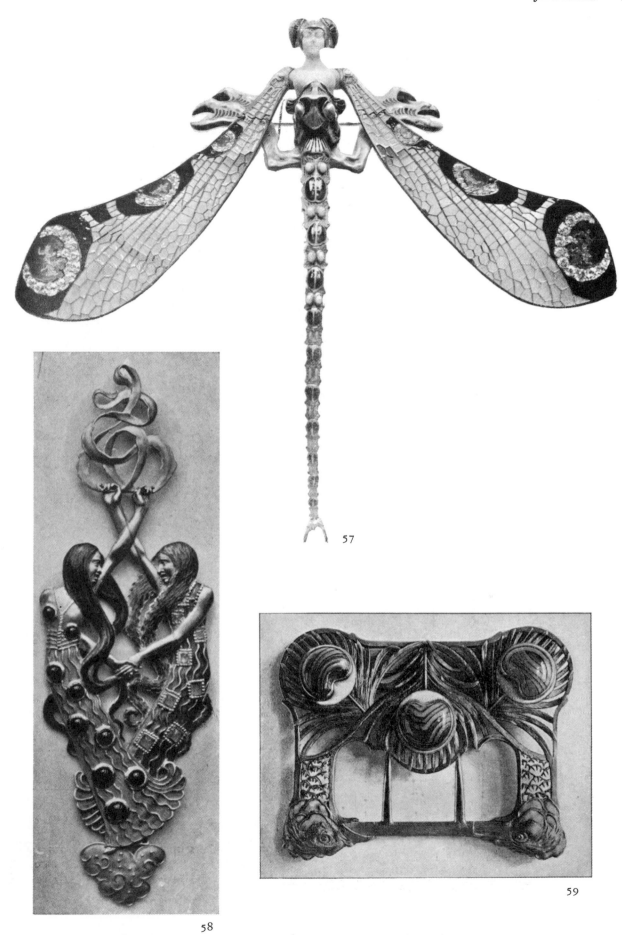

57 & 59. *Brooch and buckle, René Lalique.* 58. *Pendant, Maison Vever, design by Eugène Grasset.*

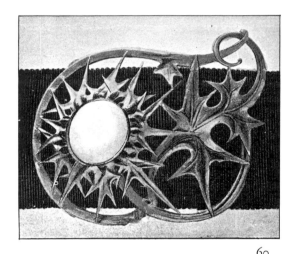

60

61

62

60 & 62. Bracelet and brooch, René Lalique.   61. Pendant, Charles Rivaud.

64

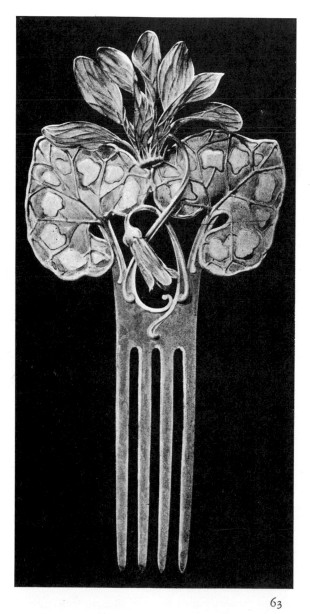

63

65

66

63. *Comb, Maison Vever.*   64. *Pendant, Edward Colonna, for L'Art Nouveau Bing.*   65. *Box, Georges de Feure.*
66. *Brooches, Paul-Emile Brandt.*

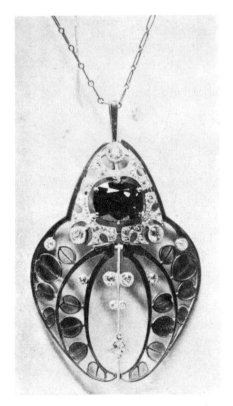

67

68

69

67 & 68. *Pendant and brooch, Maison Vever.*   69. *Pendants, Edgar Simpson.*

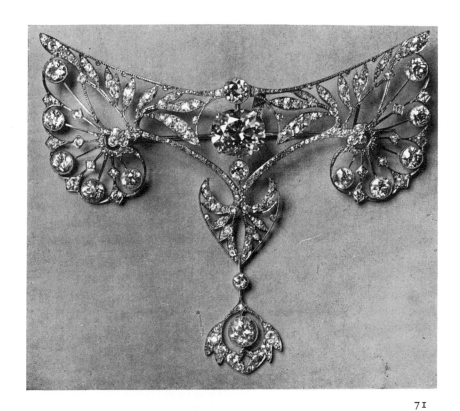

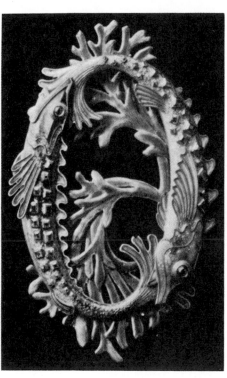

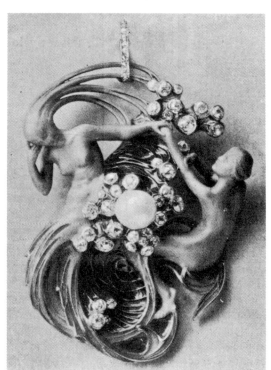

70

71

72

73

70. *Chain, Frédéric Boucheron.* 71. *Brooch, Henri Vever.* 72. *Buckle, Maison Vever, design by Eugène Grasset.*
73. *Necklace, Maison Vever.*

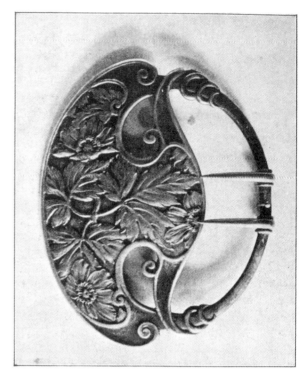

74

75

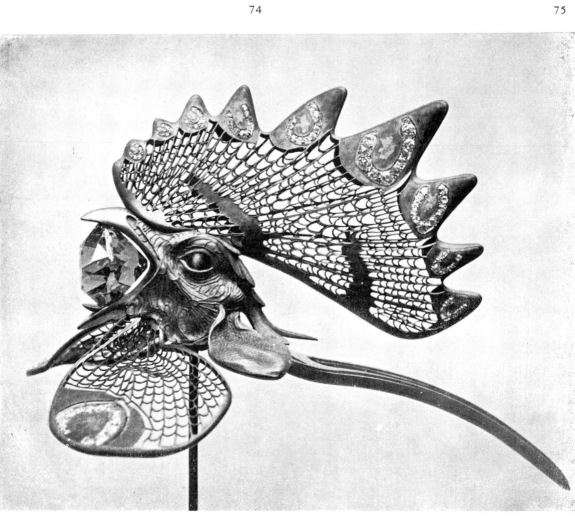

76

74. *Jewelry box, Antoine (Tony) Garnier.*   75 & 76. *Buckle and hatpin, René Lalique.*

77

78

79

80

77. *Pendant, Frédéric Boucheron.*   78. *Buckle, Mme Guffroy.*   79. *Hatpin, René Lalique.*
80. *Pendants, brooches and buckle, Théodore Lambert.*

81

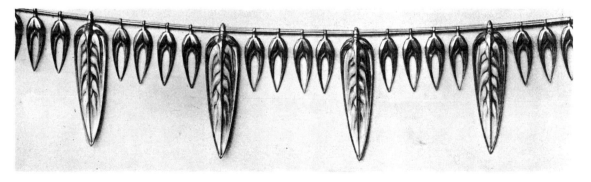

82

81. *Pendant, Georges Fouquet.*   82. *Necklace, Lucien Gaillard.*

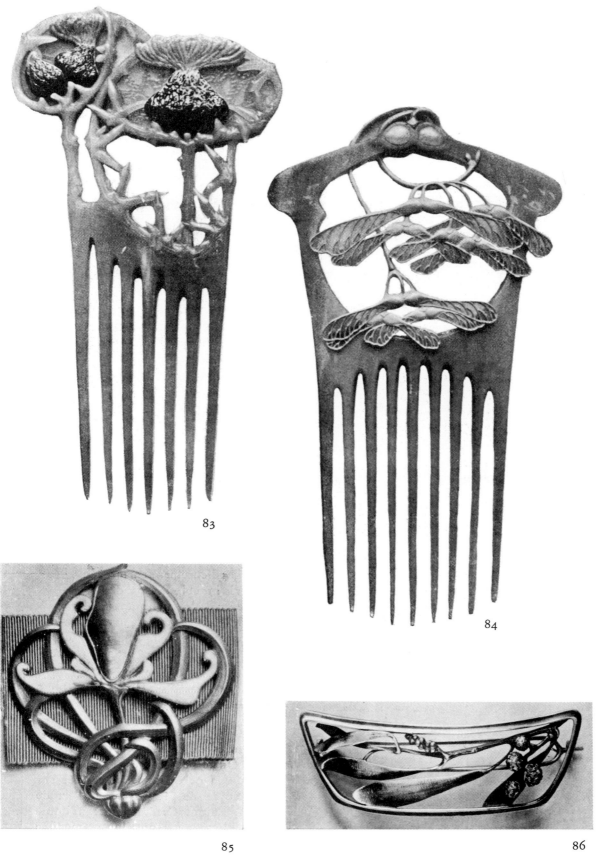

83 & 84. *Combs, René Lalique.*   85. *Buckle, Edward Colonna, for L'Art Nouveau Bing.*
86. *Brooch, Paul-Emile Brandt.*

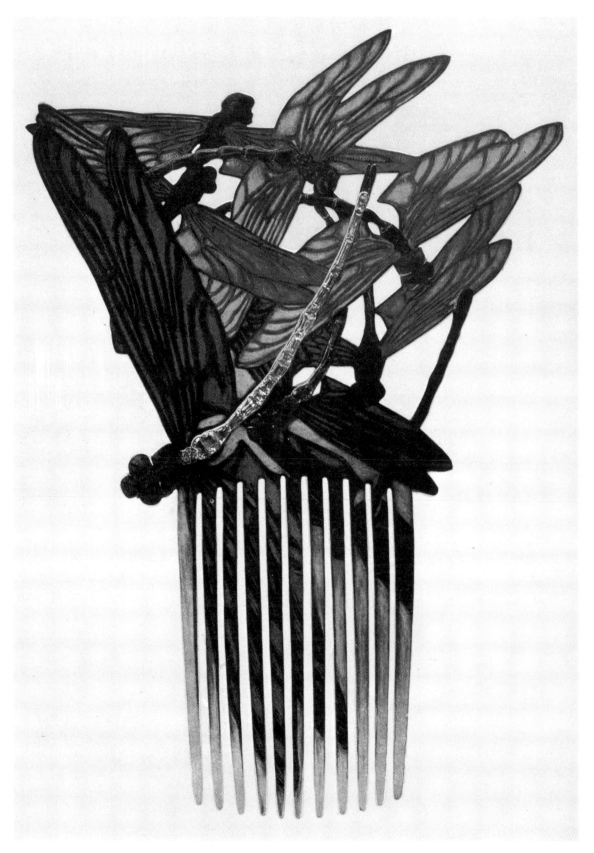

87

87. Comb, René Lalique.

METALWORK

88

88. *Staircase railing, Emile Robert.*

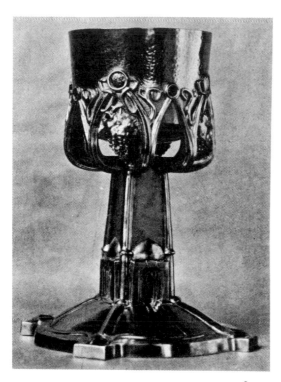

89

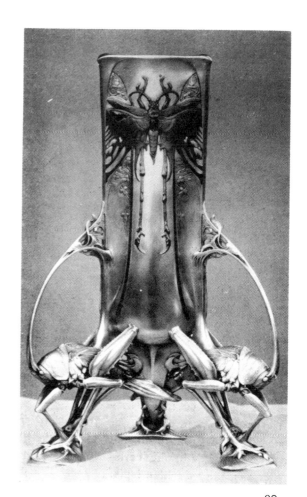

90

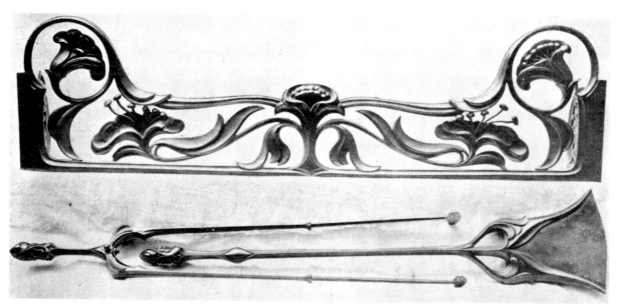

91

89. *Goblet, Alexander Fisher.*   90. *Silver vase, Jules Auguste Habert-Dys.*   91. *Fireplace accessories, Abel Landry.*

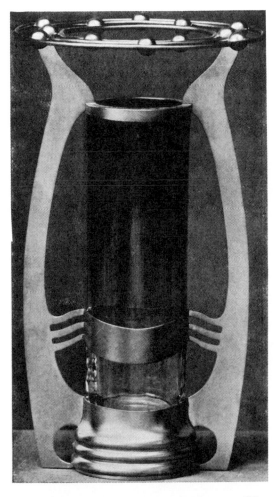

92

93

94

92. Vase, Mlle Krasnik.   93. Pitcher, Alexander Fisher.   94. Cream and sugar bowls, Carlo Bugatti.

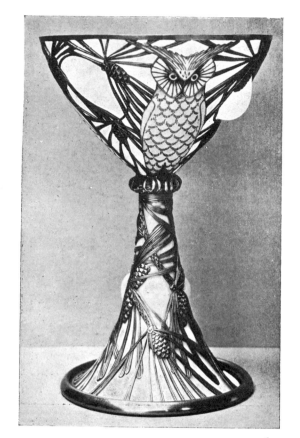

96

95

97

95. *Door handle and keyhole plate, Elisa Beetz-Charpentier.*   96. *Silver and crystal vase, Eugène Feuillâtre.*
97. *Copper vase, Jean Dunand.*

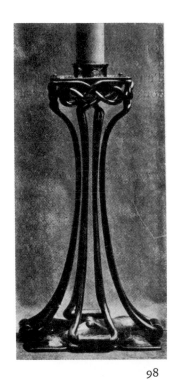

98

99

100

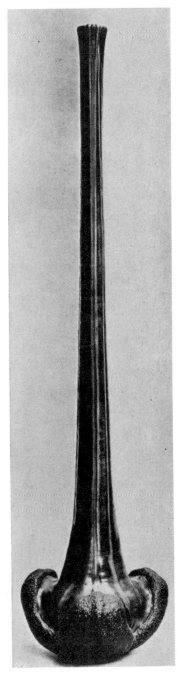

101

98. Candlestick, Richard Llewelyn Benson Rathbone.   99. Goblet, Alexander Fisher.   100. Plate, Mathieu Gallerey.
101. Vase, Lucien Gaillard.

102

103

102. Copper pitchers, Johan Thorn-Prikker.   103. Chandelier, Henri-Jules Ferdinand Bellery-Desfontaines.

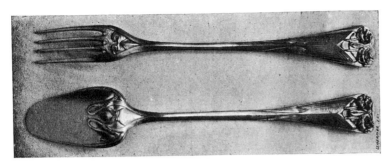

104

105

104. Flatware, Georges de Feure.   105. Brass and wrought-iron chandelier, A. G. Szabo.

106

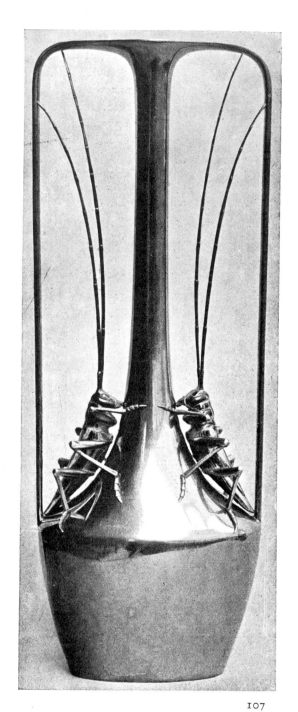

107

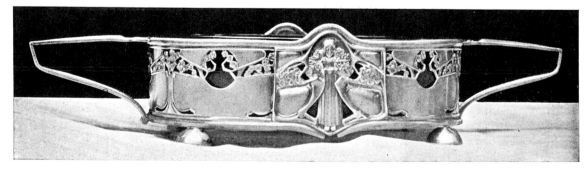

108

106. *Sword hilt, Louis Alexander Bottée.*   107. *Vase, Lucien Gaillard.*   108. *Plant holder, The Goldsmiths and Silversmiths Co., Ltd.*

109. *Chandelier, Frank Brangwyn.* 110. *Cane handle, Bréant and Coulbaux.* 111. *Keyhole plate,*
Paul Brindeau de Jarny. 112. *Candelabrum, Pierre Selmersheim.*

113

114

115

113. Cane handle, Bréant and Coulbaux.   114. Bronze vases, Lucien Gaillard.   115. Vases, Lucien Bonvallet.

116

117

118

116. *Coffee pot, Maurice Giot.* 117. *Electric heater, Regius and Paul Frank Scheidecker.*
118. *Coffee service, Lucien Gaillard.*

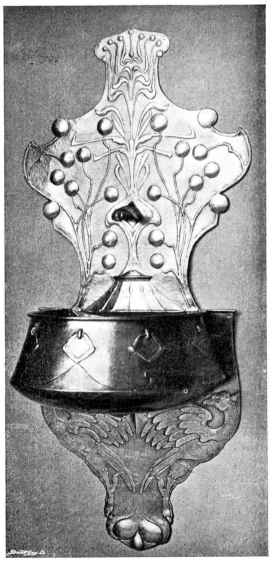

119

120

119. *Fountain, Hans Eduard von Berlepsch-Valendas.*   120. *Bronze relief, Alexandre Charpentier.*

122

121   123

121. *Bronze relief, Alexandre Charpentier.*   122. *Inkwell, Edmond Henri Becker.*
123. *Ornament for fence, Emile Robert.*

124

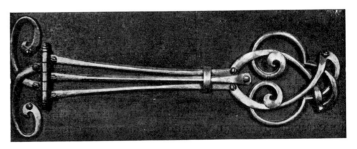

125

124. Ornament for fence, Emile Robert.   125. Hinge, Paul Brindeau de Jarny.

126

126. *Gate, Emile Robert.*

127

128

129

127. *Bronze vase, Lucien Gaillard.*   128. *Flatware, Maurice Giot.*   129. *Lamp, Henri Sauvage.*

130

131

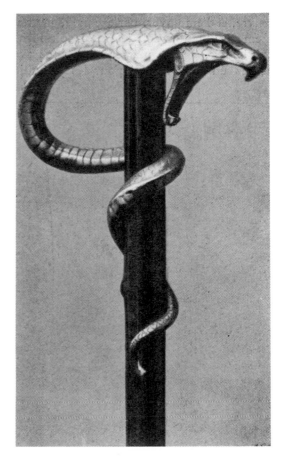

132

130. *Door handle and lock, Emile Robert.*   131. *Chandelier, Jean-Auguste Dampt.*
132. *Cane handle, Bréant and Coulbaux.*

133

134

133. Tea service, Anonymous.   134. Copper vases, Lucien Bonvallet.

135

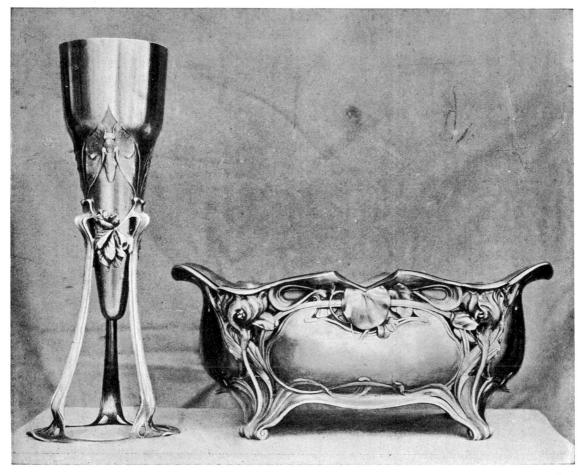

136

135. Balcony railing, Charles Plumet.   136. Goblet and vegetable dish, Bruckmann.

137

137. *Staircase railing, Edgar W. Brandt.*

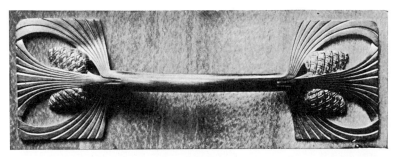

138

139

138. *Drawer handle, Léon Jallot.*   139. *Staircase railing, Louis Majorelle.*

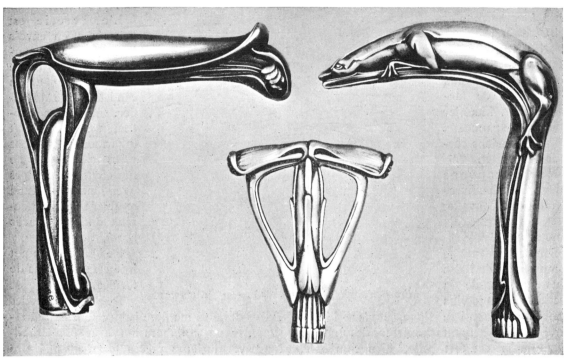

140

141

142

140. Cane handles, Georges de Feure.   141. Light fixture, Léo Laporte-Blairsy.   142. Chandelier, Tony Selmersheim.

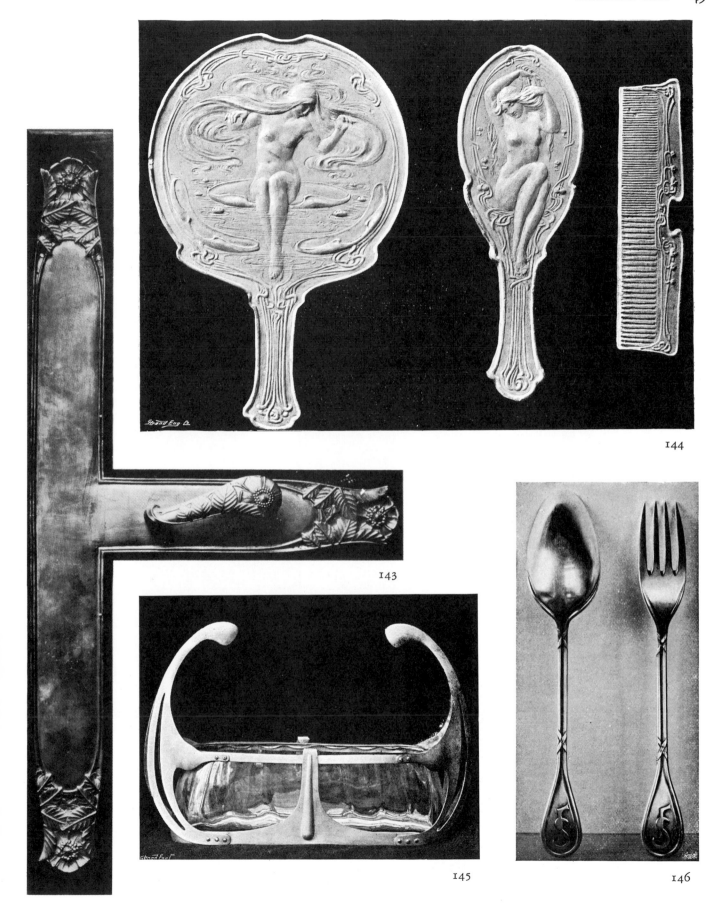

143. *Door handle, Léon Jallot.*   144. *Hand mirror, brush and comb, Mary Galway Houston.*
145. *Dish, Mlle A. Krasnik.*   146. *Flatware, Paul Frank Scheidecker.*

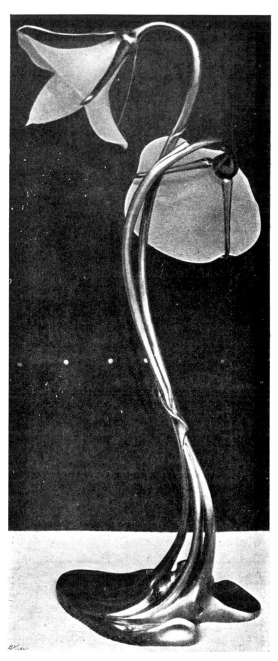

147

148

147. *Main entrance to the Castel Béranger, Hector Guimard.* 148. *Lamp, Maurice Dufrène.*

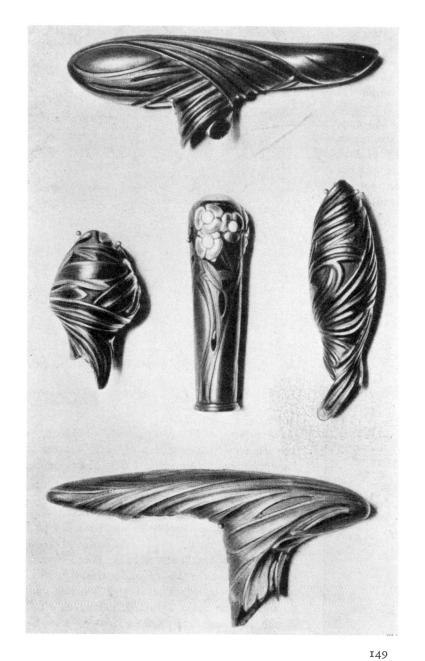

149

150

149. *Cane handles, Maurice Dufrène.*   150. *Door handle, Elisa Beetz-Charpentier.*

151

151. *Iron door, Edgar W. Brandt, design by Georges Chedanne.*

152

152. *Gate, Emile Robert, design by Georges Pradelle.*

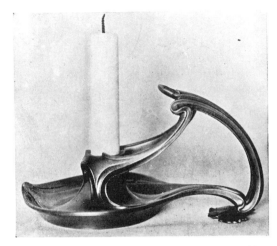

153

154

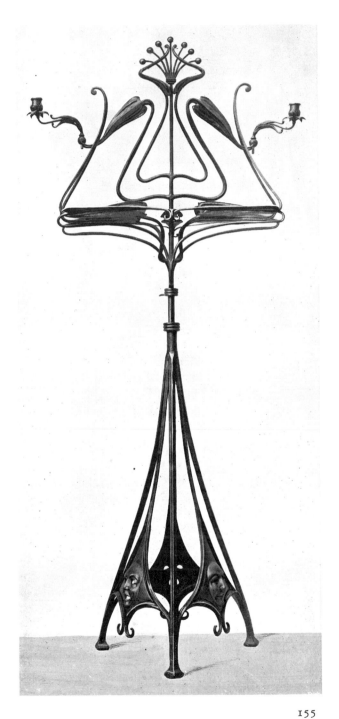

155

153. Candlestick, Maurice Giot.   154. Lamp, A. G. Szabo.   155. Music stand, Emile Robert.

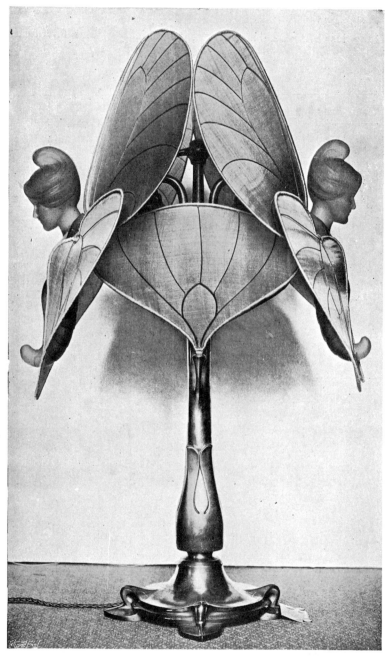

157

156

158

156. Lamp, Jean-Auguste Dampt. 157. Vase, Barboteau. 158. Silver vase with enamel, Liberty & Co.

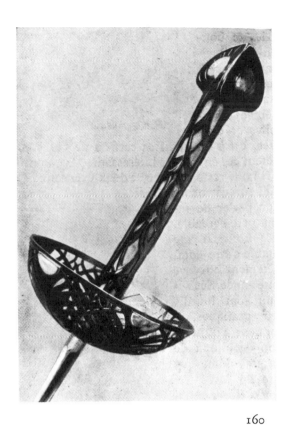

159

160

161

159. Candlestick, Charles Albert Angst.   160. Sword hilt, Lucien Gaillard.   161. Flatware, Bruckmann.

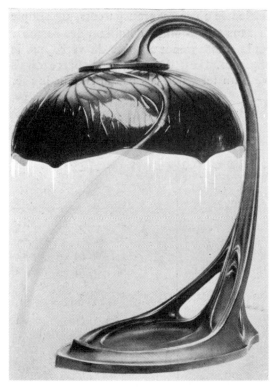

162

163

164

162. Lamp, Pierre Selmersheim.   163. Clothes hook, Paul Brindeau de Jarny.
164. Chocolate server and coffee pot, Maison Cardeilhac.

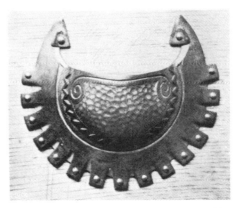

166

165   167

165. Door handle and lock, Théodore Lambert.   166. Drawer handle, Léon Jallot.   167. Vase, Lucien Bonvallet.

168

169

170

168. Sword hilt, Lucien Gaillard.   169. Vase, Jean Dunand.   170. Door handle and lock, Théodore Lambert.

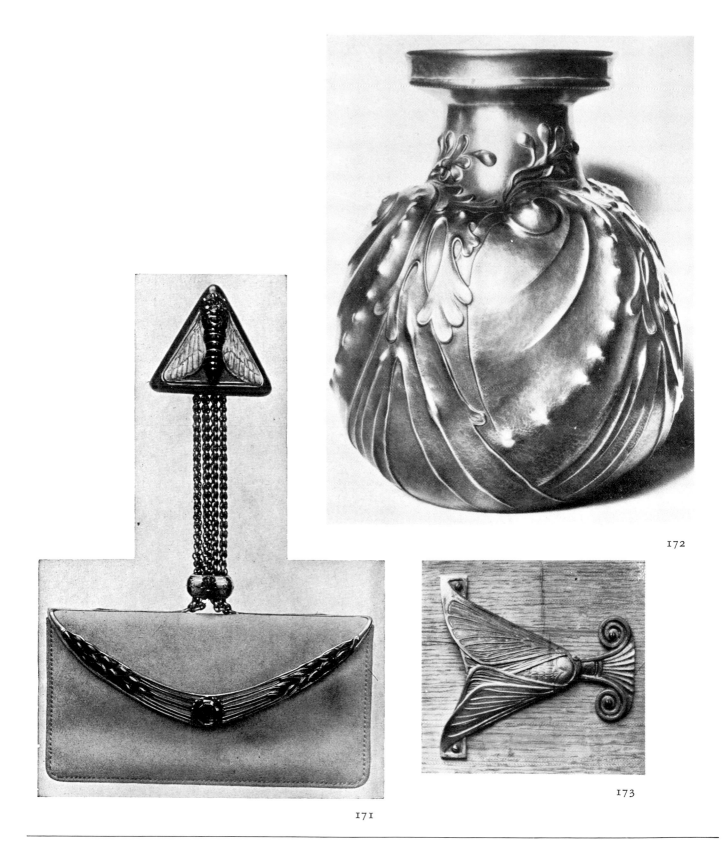

171. *Purse, Lucien Gaillard.*   172. *Copper vase, Lucien Bonvallet.*   173. *Drawer handle, Léon Jallot.*

174

175

174. Fountain, Paul Frank Scheidecker. 175. Design for watch, Alphonse Mucha.

176

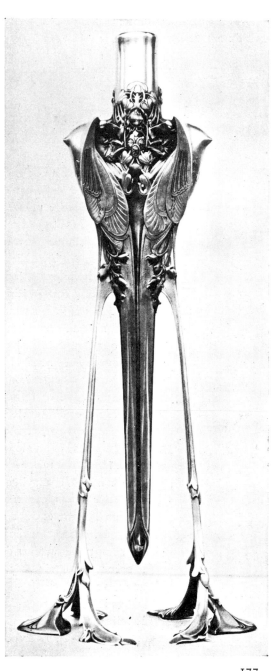

177

176. Chandelier, Maurice Dufrène.   177. Vase, Jules Auguste Habert-Dys.

178

179

178. *Clock, The Goldsmiths and Silversmiths Co., Ltd.* 179. *Lamp, Léo Laporte-Blairsy.*

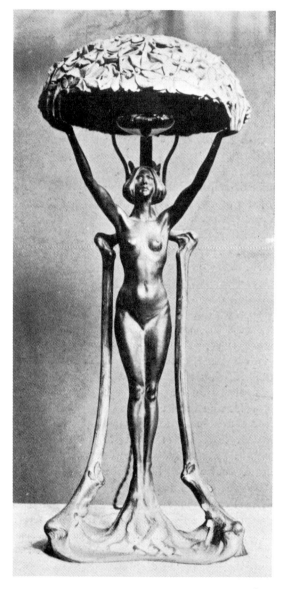

180

181

180. Lamp, Arthur Rubinstein.   181. Silver crucifix, Alexander Fisher.

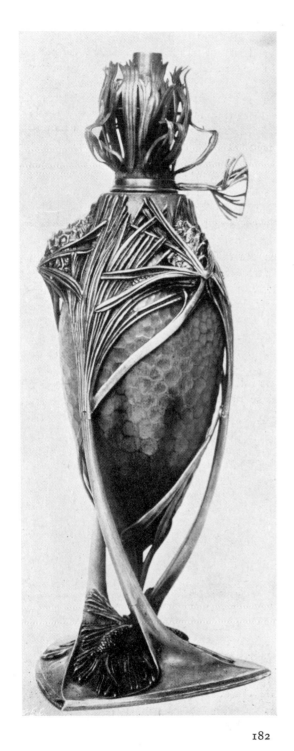

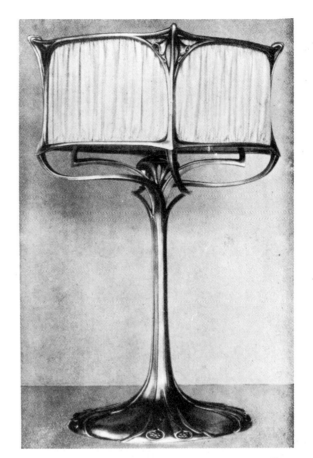

183

182

184

182. Lamp, Georges de Ribaucourt.   183. Lamp, Abel Landry.   184. Ashtray, Georges Pierre Deraisme.

185. *Door handle, Pierre Seguin.*   186. *Pitcher, Jules Auguste Habert-Dys.*   187. *Electric heater, Emile Robert.*

188

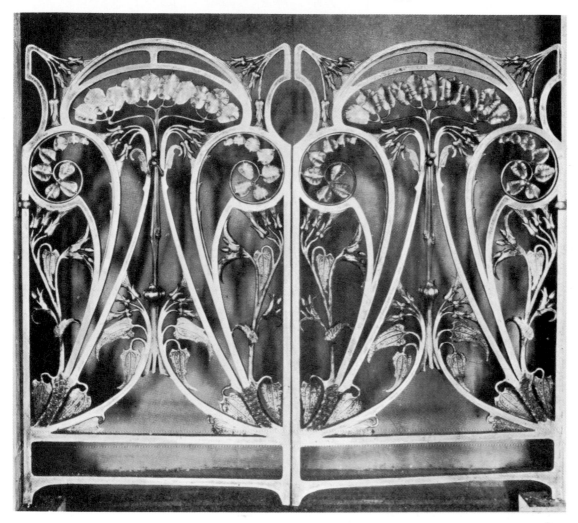

189

188. *Vegetable dish, Josef Hoffmann.* 189. *Gate, Louis Majorelle.*

190

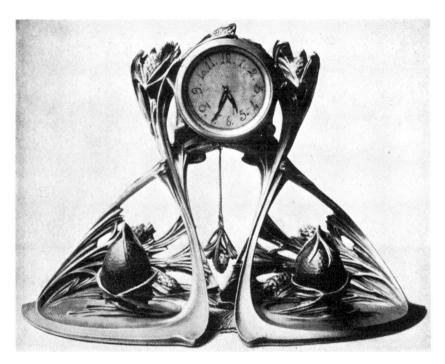

191

192

190. Candelabrum, Georges de Feure.   191. Clock and inkwell, Georges de Ribaucourt.
192. Silver relief panel, Margaret Macdonald.

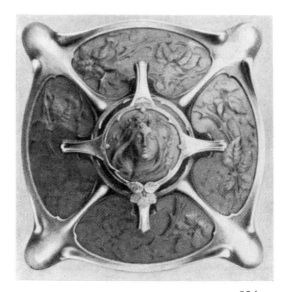

194

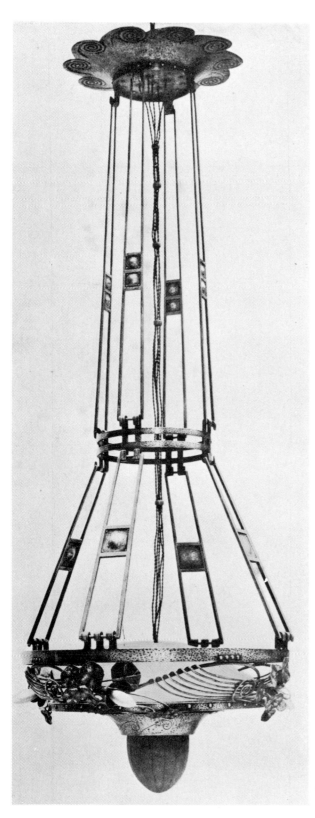

193

195

193. *Light fixture, A. G. Szabo*   194. *Inkwell (2 views), Edmond Henri Becker.*   195. *Silver cup, Liberty & Co.*

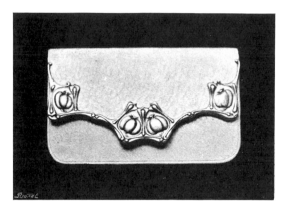

196

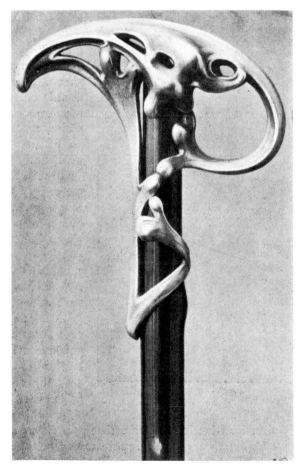

197

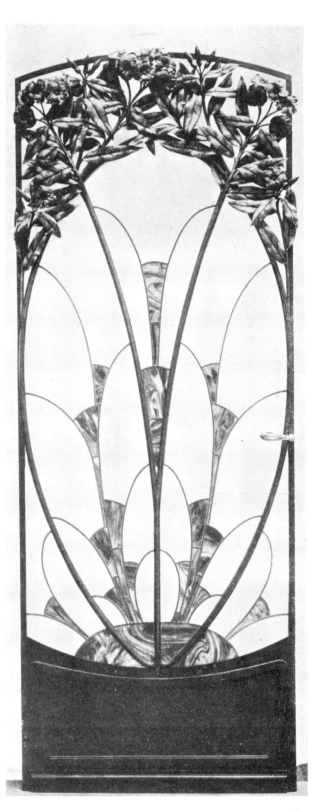

198

196. *Purse, Edward Colonna.   197. Cane handle, Bréant and Coulbaux.   198. Iron and copper door, Louis Bigaux.*

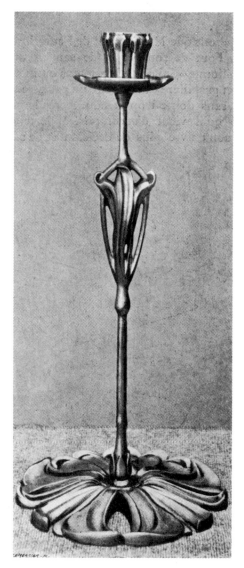

199

200

199. Gate, Victor Prouvé and Emile Robert.   200. Candlestick, Georges de Feure.

201

202

201. Vase, Lucien Gaillard.   202. Fountain, Alexandre Charpentier.

203

204

203. *Vegetable dish, Maison Cardeilhac.* 204. *Plate, Lucien Bonvallet.*

205

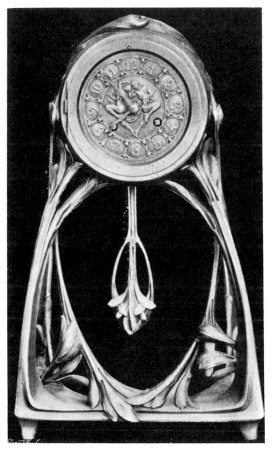

206

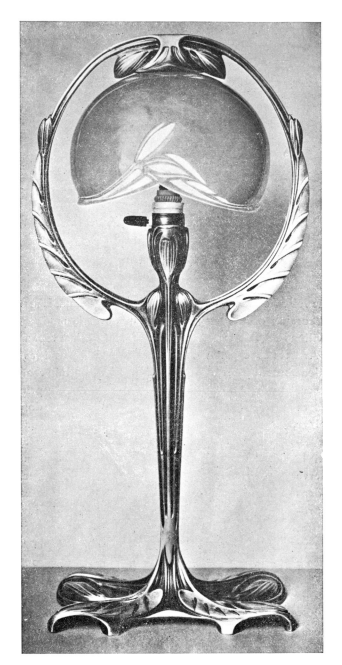

207

205. Bowl, Fleuret.   206. Clock, Camille Marc Sturbelle.   207. Lamp, Maurice Dufrène.

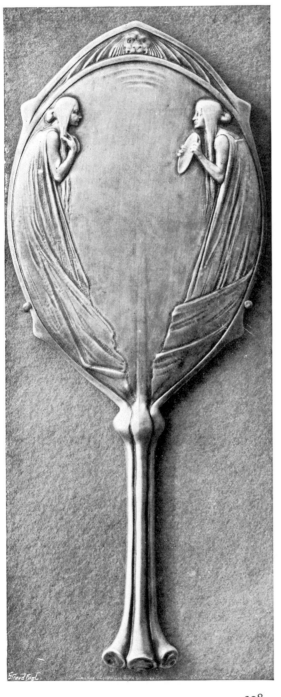

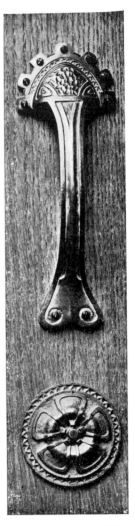

210

208

209

208. Hand mirror, Emil Meier.   209 & 210. Door and drawer handles, Léon Jallot.

211   212

214

213

211. Candelabrum, Georges de Feure.   212. Vase, Barboteau.   213. Clock, Georges de Feure.
214. Coffee pot, Eugène Lelièvre.

GLASSWARE

215. *Vase, Emile Gallé.*

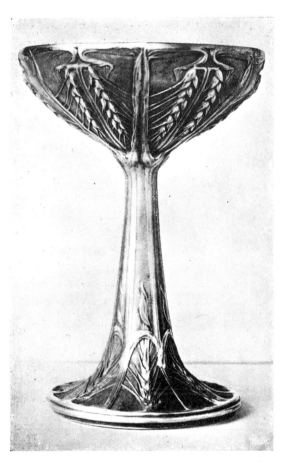

216

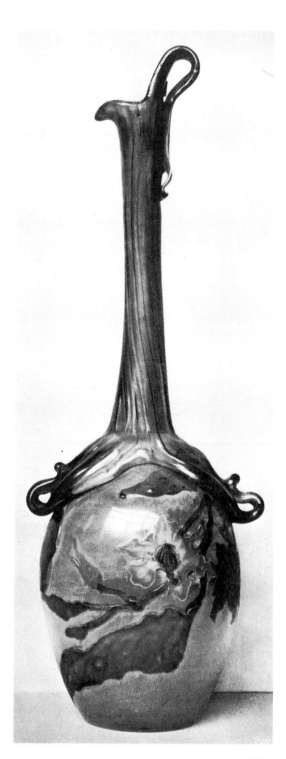

217

218

216. Goblet, René Lalique.   217. Vase, Emile Gallé.   218. Vase, Albert-Louis Dammouse.

220

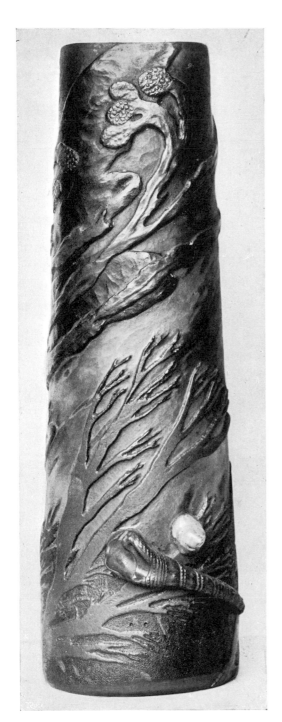

219

221

219. Vase, Emile Gallé. 220. Vase, Albert-Louis Dammouse. 221. Goblet, René Lalique.

222

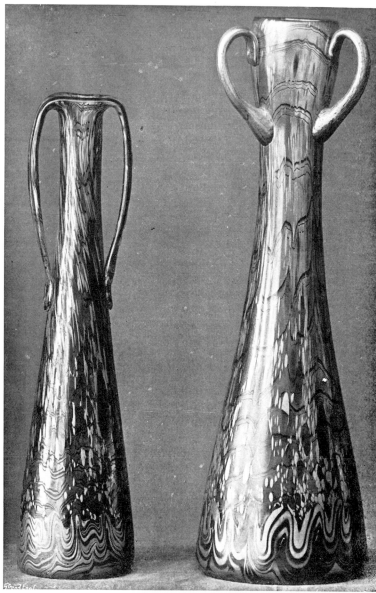

223

224

225

222. *Goblet, Koloman Moser.*   223. *Vases, Jutta Sika.*   224. *Wine glasses and carafe, James Powell and Sons.*
225. *Wine glasses, Koloman Moser.*

226

227

228

226. *Vase, Emile Gallé; ornament, Lucien Bonvallet.*   227. *Stained glass, Glasgow School of Art.*
228. *Pitcher and glasses, Gisela de Falke.*

229. *Goblet, René Lalique.*

230

230. *Vase, Emile Gallé.*

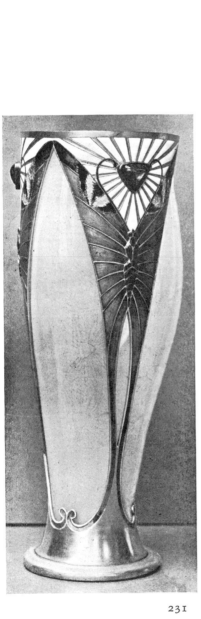

231

232

231. Vase, Eugène Feuillâtre.   232. Stained glass, Pierre Selmersheim.

234

233

235

233. *Vase, Emile Gallé.*   234. *Wine glasses, Peter Behrens.*   235. *Stained glass, Edmond Socard.*

236

237

236. Goblets, James Powell and Sons.   237. Vases, Eugène Rousseau.

238

239

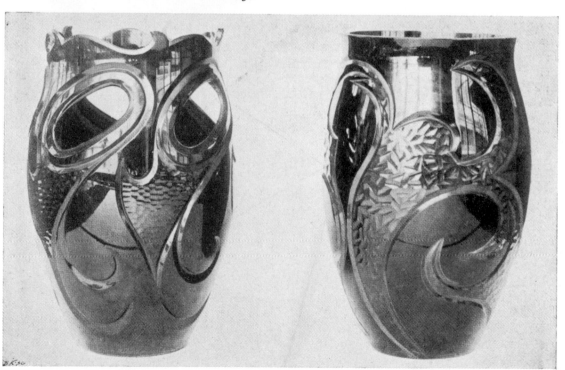

240

238. Pitcher, Koloman Moser.   239. Vases, Karl Koepping.   240. Vases, Val Saint-Lambert.

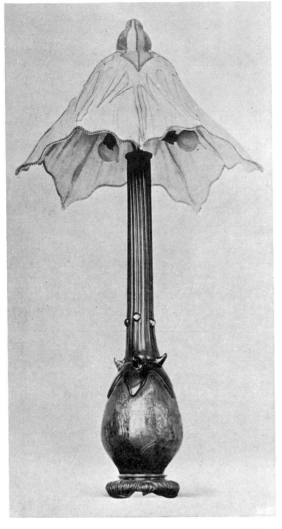

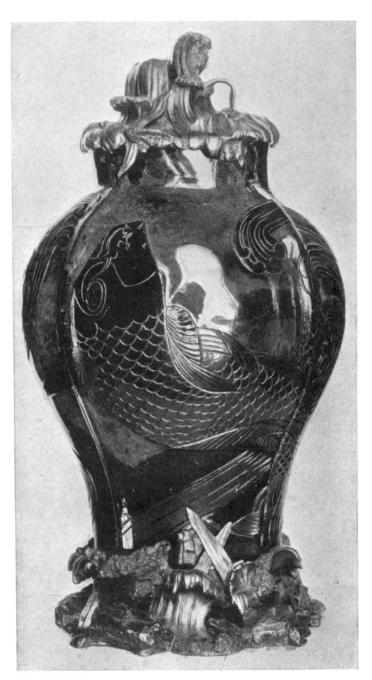

241   242

241. Lamp, Emile Gallé.   242. Vase, Ernest Michel Levillé.

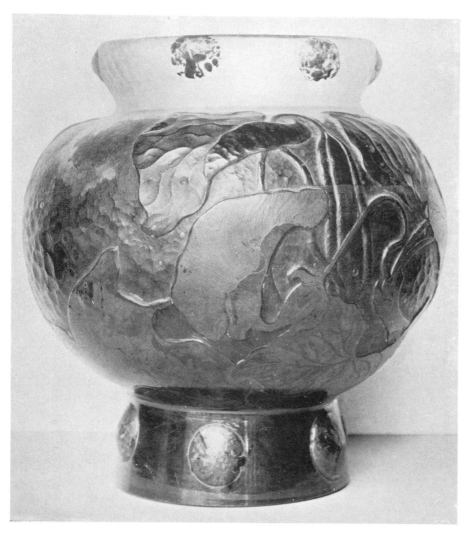

243

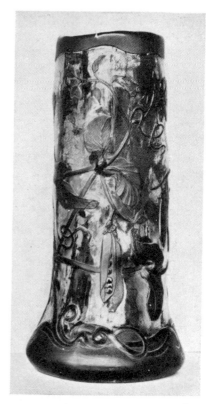

244

245

243. *Vase, Emile Gallé.* 244 & 245. *Vase and pitcher with glasses, Ernest Michel Leveillé and Eugène Rousseau.*

246

246. Stained glass, Farmakowsky.

247

247. *Stained glass, Paul Albert Besnard.*

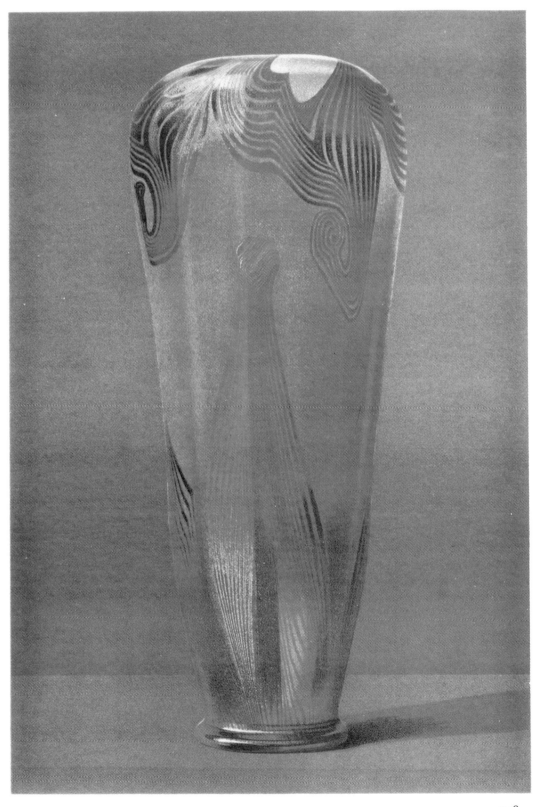

248

248. *Vase, Louis Comfort Tiffany.*

249

250

251

252

249. *Goblets, James Powell and Sons.* 250. *Vase, Albert-Louis Dammouse.* 251 & 252. *Vases, Emile Gallé.*

253

254

255

253. *Carafe, goblet and pitcher, Edward Michel Leveillé.*   254. *Pitcher, Koloman Moser.*
255. *Carafes, James Powell and Sons.*

256

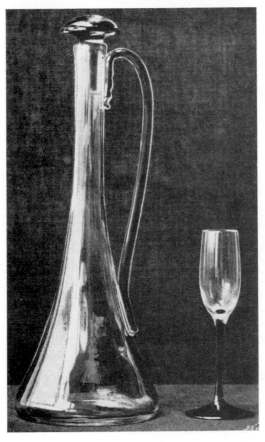

257

258

256. Carafe and glasses, Edward Colonna. 257. Carafe and goblet, Koloman Moser. 258. Vase, Emile Gallé.

259

259. Vases, Louis Comfort Tiffany.

260. *Stained glass, Félix Gaudin.*

261

262

263

261. Stained glass, Gustave Serrurier-Bovy.   262. Vase, Emile Gallé.   263. Vases, Louis Comfort Tiffany.

PORCELAIN
AND POTTERY

264

264. Vases, E. Gérard.

265

266

267

265. Vase, Auguste Delaherche; ornament, Lucien Bonvallet.   266. Coffee service, Georges de Feure.
267. Vase, Ernest Chaplet.

268

269

268. *Vases, Ernest Chaplet.*   269. *Vases, Albert-Louis Dammouse.*

270

271

270. *Vase and ornament, Lucien Gaillard.*   271. *Vases, Albert-Louis Dammouse.*

272

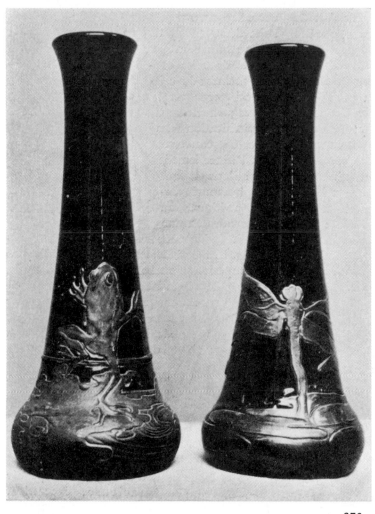

273

274

72. *Vases, Alfred William Finch.*   273. *Vases, Rookwood.*   274. *Vase, Lucien Bonvallet, for Maison Cardeilhac.*

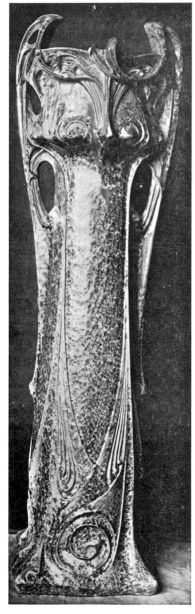

275

276

275. Vase, Eugène Guimard.   276. Vase, Royal Copenhagen.

277

278

279

277. *Vase, Ernest Chaplet.* 278. *Vase, Lucien Gaillard.* 279. *Vases, Max Läuger.*

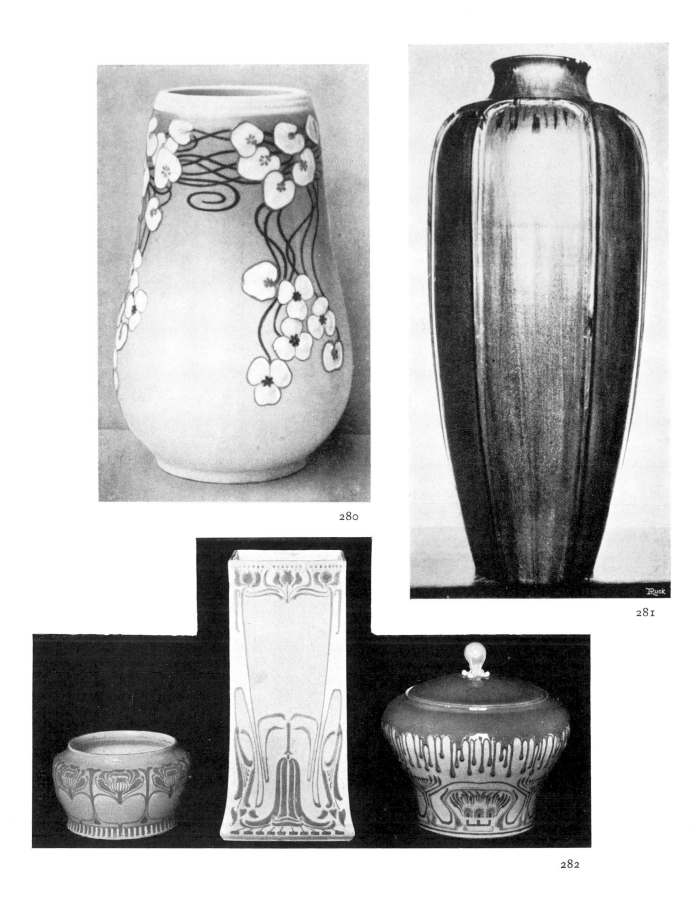

280

281

282

280. *Vase, Bing and Groendhal.*   281. *Vase, Auguste Delaherche.*   282. *Vase and containers, Georges de Feure.*

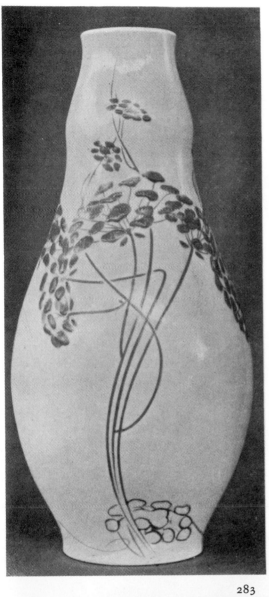

284

283

285

286

283. Vase, Sèvres.   284. Vase, Ernest Chaplet.   285. Vase, Glatigny.   286. Vases, Niels Hansen-Jacobsen.

287

287. *Fountain, Georges Hoentschel.*

288

288. *Fountain, Max Läuger.*

289

290

291

289. *Vases, Glatigny.*   290. *Fountain, Glatigny.*   291. *Vases, Elisabeth Schmidt-Pecht, for* La Maison Moderne.

292

293

294

292. *Vase, Emile Decoeur.*   293. *Pitcher, Albert-Louis Dammouse.*   294. *Vases, Adrien Pierre Dalpayrat.*

295

296

295. Cup, Auguste Delaherche; ornament, Lucien Bonvallet.   296. Vases, Georges de Feure.

297

298

297. Coffee service, Rozenburg.   298. Vases, Etienne Moreau-Nélaton.

300

299

301

299. *Vase, Rozenburg.*   300. *Vase, Auguste Delaherche.*   301. *Coffee and tea service, Maurice Dufrène.*

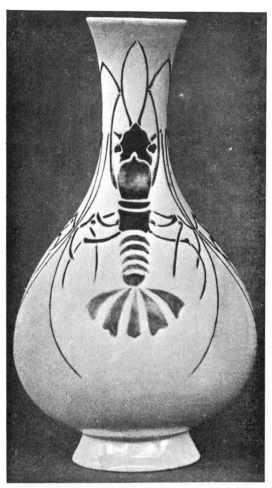

302

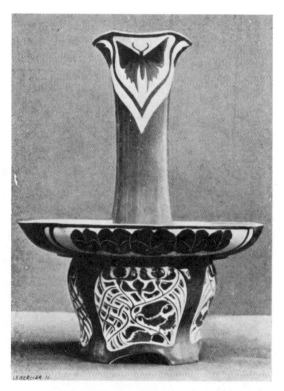

303

304

302. *Vase, Sèvres.*   303. *Vase, Theodor Hermann Schmuz-Baudisz.*   304. *Coffee service, Meissen.*

305   306

307

305. Vase, Auguste Delaherche.   306. Vase, Edward Colonna.   307. Vases, Grueby.

TEXTILES

308. *Lace fan, Mathurin Méheut.*

309

310

309. *Fabric design, Liberty & Co.*   310. *Rug, Frank Brangwyn.*

311

312

313

311. Rug, Edward Colonna.   312. Fabric design, Georges de Feure.   313. Rug, Koloman Moser.

315

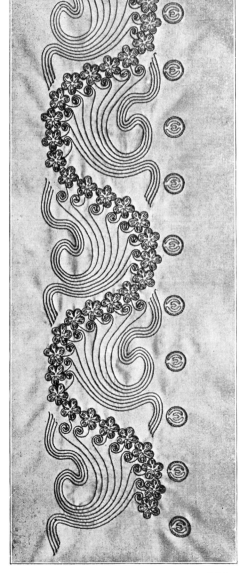

314

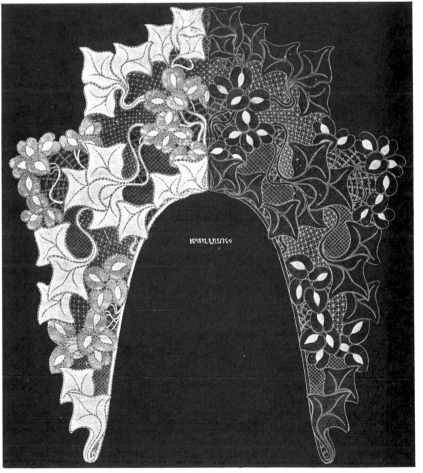

316

314. Embroidery, Anonymous Viennese.   315. Batik tea-cozy, Mlle Morice.   316. Lace, Karl Vleck.

317

318

317. Lace, Karl Vleck.   318. Batik cushion, Mlle Morice.

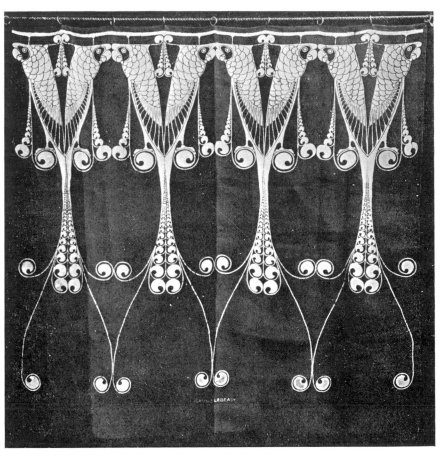

319

320

319. Batik hanging, Joris Johannes Christiaan Lebeau.   320. Embroidery, Eugène Belville.

321

322

323

321. Lace, Maurice Dufrène.   322. Fabric design, Georges de Feure.   323. Embroidered pillow, Edme Couty.

324

325

324. *Embroidered tablecloth, Ann Macbeth.*   325. *Embroidered panel, Glasgow School of Art.*

326

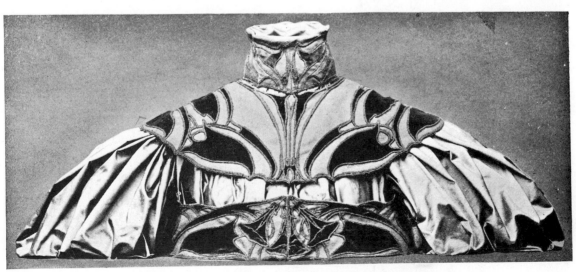

327

326. *Painted frieze on silk, Charles Plumet and Tony Selmersheim.*   327. *Embroidered blouse, Mme P. Rivière.*

328

329

330

328. *Embroidered tea-cozy, Glasgow School of Art.*   329. *Fabric design, Liberty & Co.*
330. *Embroidered gown, Mme Ory-Robin.*

331

332

331. Embroidered panel, Ann Macbeth.   332. Embroidered blouse, Mme P. Rivière.

333

334

333. Embroidered tablecloth, Jules Coudyser.   334. Batik tea-cozy, Joris Johannes Christiaan Lebeau.

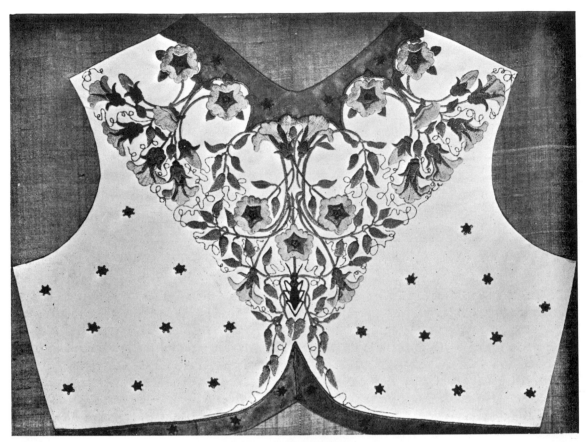

335

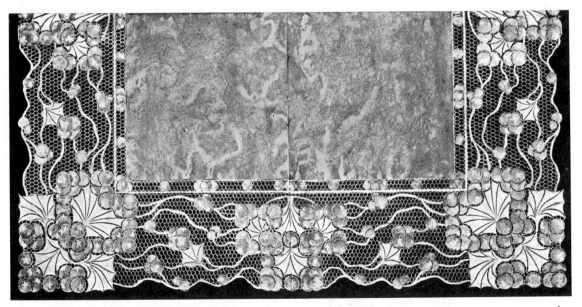

336

335. *Embroidered vest, Mlle Morisset.*   336. *Lace, Karl Vleck.*

337

337. *Lace, Anonymous Viennese.*

338

338. *Embroidered hanging, Edme Couty.*

339

340

341

339. *Embroidered handbag, Eugène Belville.*   340. *Tapestry, Sherrebek.*   341. *Fabric design, Edme Couty.*

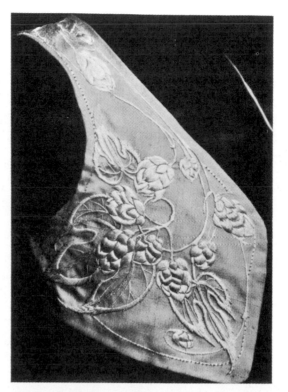

343

344

342. *Embroidery, Lucien Bonvallet.*   343. *Embroidered vest, Victor Lheur.*   344. *Tapestry, Paul Elie Ranson.*

345

346

345 & 346. Rugs, Ginzkey.

347

348

349

347. *Tapestry, Sherrebek, design by Otto Eckmann.*   348. *Embroidered handbag, Gabriel Prévot.*
349. *Woven fabric, Koloman Moser.*

350

351

352

350. *Rug, Koloman Moser.*   351. *Embroidered pillow, Glasgow School of Art.*   352. *Lace, Gabriel Prévot.*

ARCHITECTURE

353

353. *Louis Majorelle's villa at Nancy, Henri Sauvage.*

354.

354

354. *Restaurant "Le Pavillon Bleu," E. A. R. Dulong and Gustave Serrurier-Bovy.*

355

355. *Pavillon Bleu at the Paris World's Fair, 1900, E. A. R. Dulong.*

356

357

356. *Façade of the Pavillon Bleu at the Paris World's Fair, 1900, E. A. R. Dulong.*
357. *Restaurant façade, Charles Plumet and Tony Selmersheim.*

MAISON   A. NIGUET

358

359

358. *Store façade, Paul Hankar.*   359. *Bedroom, Charles Plumet and Tony Selmersheim.*

360. Dining room, Charles Plumet and Tony Selmersheim.

361

361. *Sitting room, Mackay Hugh Baillie-Scott.*

362

363

362. *Dining room fireplace, Charles Plumet and Tony Selmersheim.*   363. *René Lalique's townhouse, René Lalique.*

364

365

364. *Façade of house, Charles Plumet.*   365. *Door of a shop in Brussels, Paul Hankar.*

366

366. Dining room. Paintings, Henri Martin. Woodwork, Henri Rapin.
Furniture, Henri-Jules Ferdinand Bellery-Desfontaines.

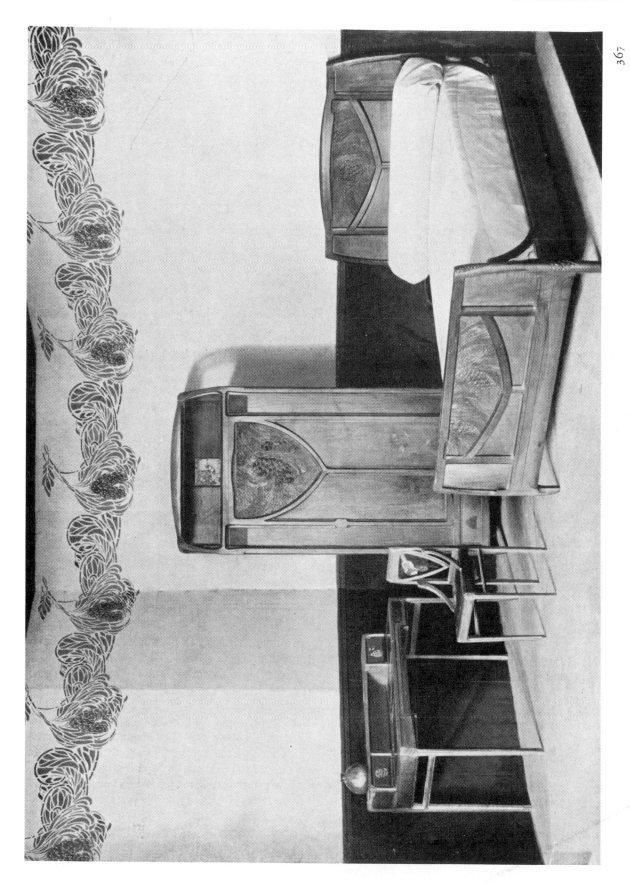

367

367. *Bedroom, E. A. Seguy.*

368

369

368. Store façade, F. Dufat.   369. Villa, Charles Plumet.

370

370. *Store façade in Paris, Léon Lebègue.*

371

371. *Dining room, Ludwig Hohlwein.*

372. *Dining room. Paintings, Henri Martin. Woodwork, Henri Rapin.*
Furniture, Henri-Jules Ferdinand Bellery-Desfontaines.

373. *Salon fireplace, Tony Selmersheim.*

374

375

374. Bedroom, Maurice Dufrène.   375. Study, Tony Selmersheim.

376

376. Hall, Tony Selmersheim.

377

377. *Dining room, Abel Landry.*

378. *Study, Paul Follot.*

379

379. *Dining room, Bruno Paul.*

380

381

380. *Vestibule of the Castel Béranger, Hector Guimard.*   381. *Maison Tassel in Brussels, Victor Horta.*

382

383

382. *Paul Hankar's townhouse in Brussels, Paul Hankar.*   383. *Store façade, Maurice Biais.*

384. *Bedroom, Charles Plumet and Tony Selmersheim.*

385. *Entrance to the 1902 Turin Exposition, Raimondo D'Aronco.*

386. *Vestibule of the German section at the Turin Exposition, Peter Behrens.*

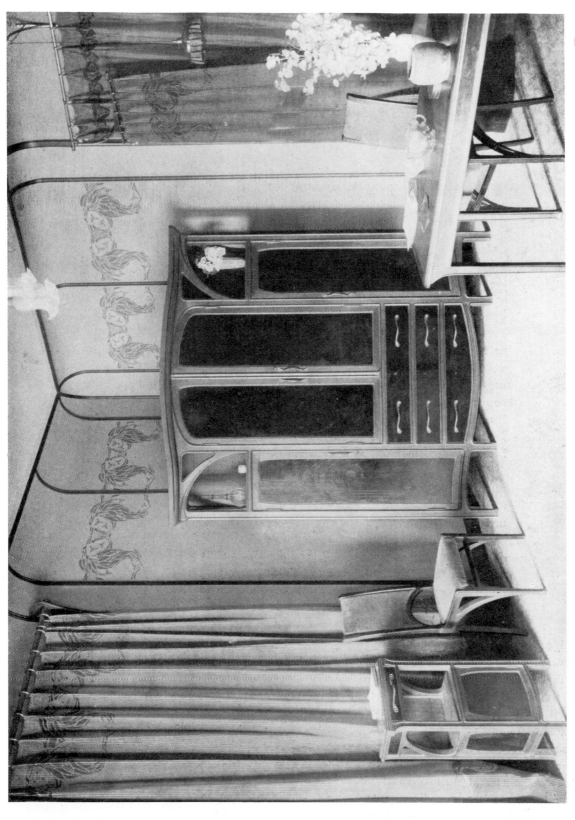

387. *Bedroom, Maurice Dufrène.*

388

388. *Apartment building, Georges Chedanne.*

389

389. *Store façade, Tony Selmersheim.*

390

390. *Bedroom, Paul Follot.*

391. *Dining room, Maurice Dufrène.*

392. *Study, Louis Félix Bigaux.*

393

393. *Dining room, Victor Horta.*

394. *Sitting room, Gustave Serrurier-Bovy.*

395

395. *Restaurant, Louis Félix Bigaux.*

396

396. *Dining room, Gustave Serrurier-Bovy.*

397

397. *Furnishings for a corner fireplace, Hans Eduard von Berlepsch-Valendas.*

398

399

398. Dining room, Victor Horta.   399. Library, Tony Selmersheim.

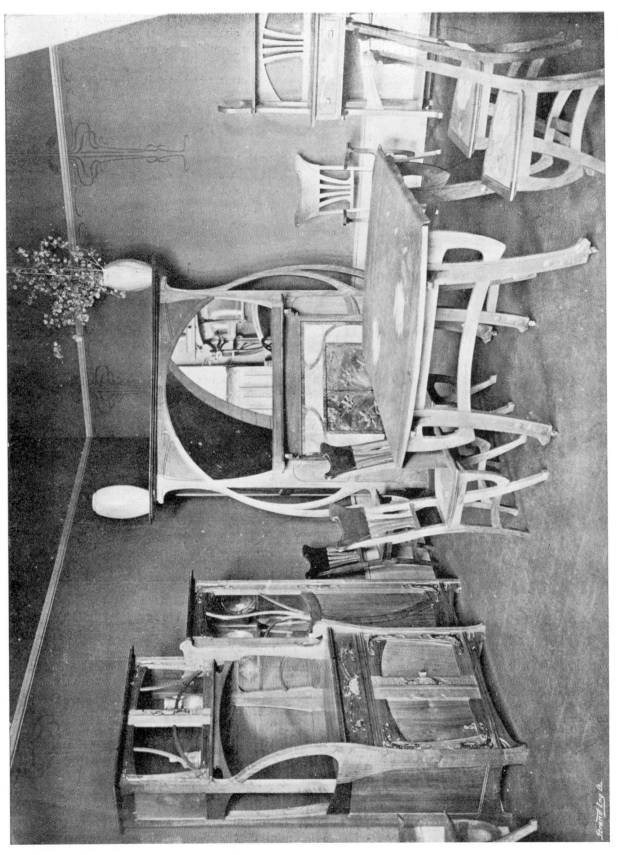

400. *Dining room, Gustave Serrurier-Bovy.*

401. *Hall and music room, Gesellius, Lindgren and Saarinen.*

402

403

402. *Hall, Josef Hoffmann.*   403. *Sitting room, Herbert MacNair and Frances Macdonald MacNair.*

404

405

404. Furnishings for a corner fireplace, Mackay Hugh Baillie-Scott.   405. Bar, Ludwig Hohlwein.

406. Wall in billiard room, Eugène Vallin.

407. *Library, Maurice Dufrène.*

408

408. *Bedroom, Maurice Dufrène.*

409. *Main entrance to Paris World's Fair, 1900, René Binet.*

410

411

410. *Dining room, Bruno Paul.*   411. *Furnishings for a corner fireplace, Théodore Lambert.*

412

413

412. *Hall, Josef Hoffmann.* 413. *Sitting room. Furniture, Charles Rennie Mackintosh. Decoration, George Walton.*

414

414. Fireplace in a billiard room, George Walton.

415

415. Bedroom, Gustave Serrurier-Bovy.

416

417

416. *Dining room, Josef Hoffmann.*   417. *Louis Majorelle's villa at Nancy, Henri Sauvage.*

418

419

418. *Dining-room table and chairs, Henry van de Velde.*   419. *Dining room, Louis Félix Bigaux.*

420

420. Bank, Gesellius, Lindgren and Saarinen.

421

421. *Fireplace, Henri-Jules Ferdinand Bellery-Desfontaines.*

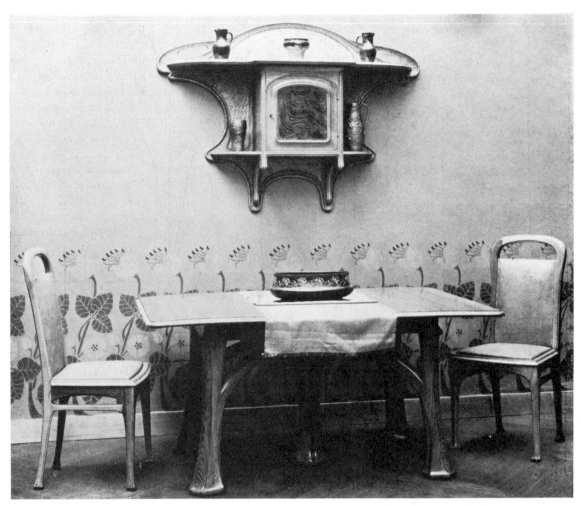

422

423

422. *Dining room, Maurice Pillard-Verneuil.*   423. *Austrian villa, Ludwig Baumann.*

424

425

424. *Country house, Emile André.*   425. *Study, Victor Horta.*

426

426. *Study, Maurice Dufrène.*

427. *Austrian villa at the Turin Exposition, Ludwig Baumann.*

428

428. *Private home, Charles Plumet.*

429. *Dining-room fireplace, Henri-Jules Ferdinand Bellery-Desfontaines.*

FURNITURE

430. Buffet, Maurice Dufrène.

431

432

431. *Buffet, Henri-Jules Ferdinand Bellery-Desfontaines.*   432. *Tea table, Abel Landry.*

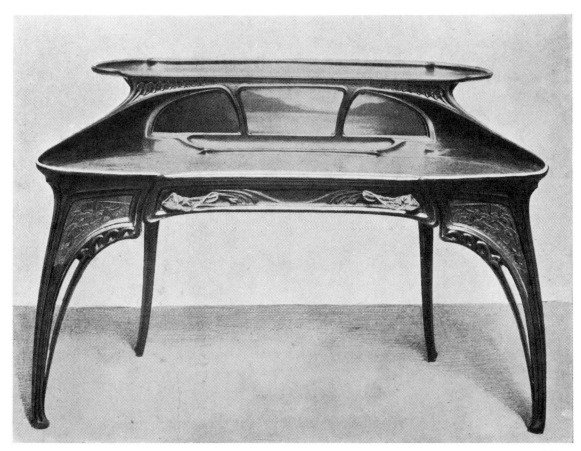

433

434

433. Desk, Jacques Gruber.   434. Buffet, Eugène Gaillard.

435

436

435 & 436. Cabinet and armoire, Louis Majorelle.

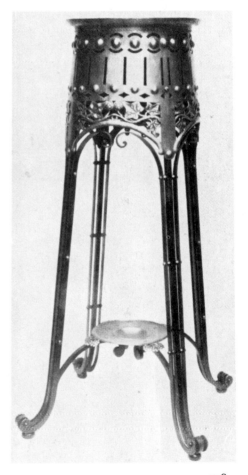

437

438

437. *Sofa, Tony Selmersheim.*   438. *Plant stand, Emile Robert.*

439

440

439. Music cabinet, Alexandre Charpentier.   440. Armoire, Gesellius, Lindgren and Saarinen.

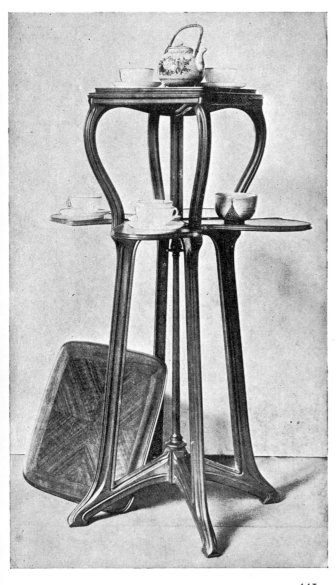

441

442

441. *Tea table, Eugène Gaillard.*   442. *Etagère, Emile Gallé.*

443

444

443. Table and lamp, Emile Gallé.   444. Foyer screen, Charles Albert Gautier.

445

446

245. *Armoire, Maurice Pillard-Verneuil.   446. Buffet, Maurice Dufrène.*

447

448

447. *Bed and night table, Louis Majorelle.*   448. *Buffet, Gustave Serrurier-Bovy.*

449

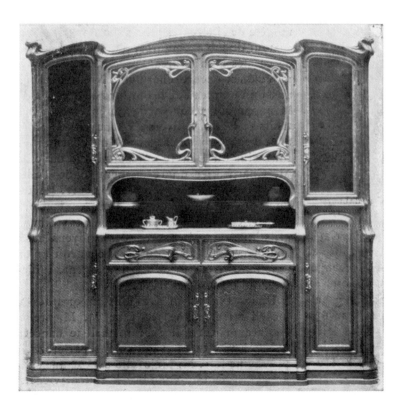

450

449. Desk, Abel Landry.   450. Cabinet, Eugène Gaillard.

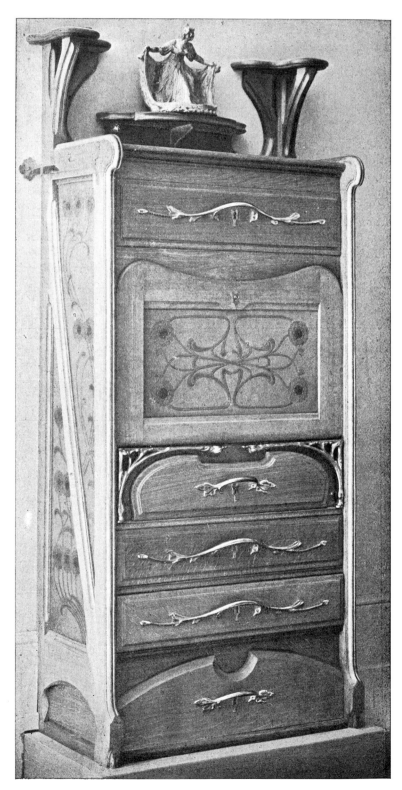

451   452

451. *Tea table, Abel Landry.*   452. *Secretary, Louis Benouville.*

453

453. *Armoire, Henri-Jules Ferdinand Bellery-Desfontaines.*

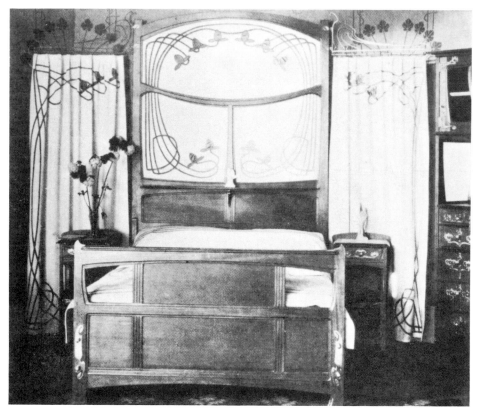

454

455

454. *Bed, Gustave Serrurier-Bovy.* 455. *Buffet, Charles Albert Angst.*

456

457

456. *Chair, Edward Colonna.   457. Tea table, Théodore Lambert.*

458

459

458. *Bookcase, Pierre Selmersheim.* 459. *Armchair, Charles Plumet and Tony Selmersheim.*

460

461

460. *Buffet, Charles Albert Angst.*   461. *Buffet, Louis Majorelle.*

462

463

462. *Dining-room table and chairs, Léon Jallot.*   463. *Chaise longue, Tony Selmersheim.*

464

465

464. Cabinet, Charles Robert Ashbee.   465. Table and chair, Charles Plumet and Tony Selmersheim.

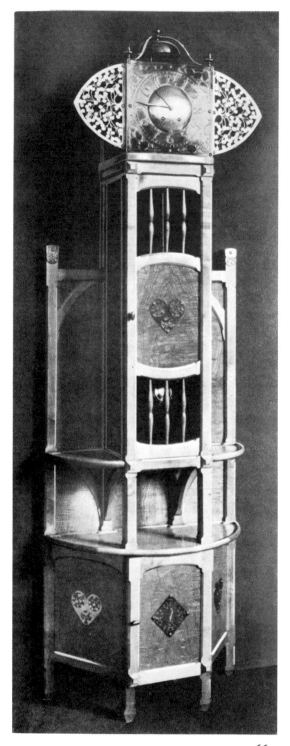

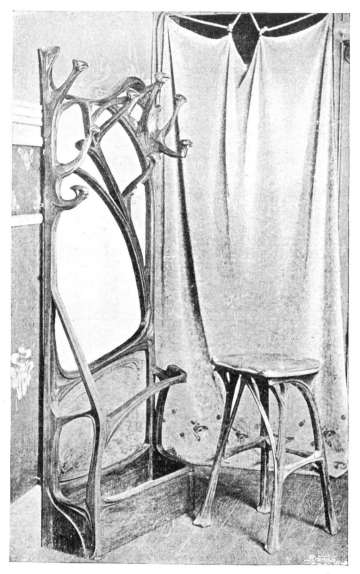

466

467

466. *Clock, Paul Frank Scheidecker.*   467. *Umbrella stand and chair, Hector Guimard.*

468

469

468. *Buffet, Gustave Serrurier-Bovy.*   469. *Tea table, Eugène Gaillard.*

470

470. *Cabinet, Emile Gallé.*

471

471. *Buffet, Tony Selmersheim.*

472

473

472. *Dining-room ensemble, Charles Plumet and Tony Selmersheim.*   473. *Dining-room table and chair,*
Louis Majorelle.

474

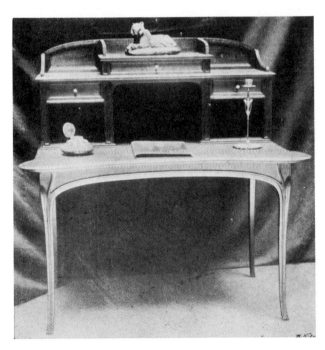

475

474. *Dresser, Louis Majorelle.* 475. *Desk, Georges de Feure.*

476

476. *Buffet, Hans Eduard von Berlepsch-Valendas.*

477

477. *Serving table, Charles Plumet and Tony Selmersheim.*

478

479

478. *Sofa, Edward Colonna.*   479. *Buffet, Henri Sauvage.*

480

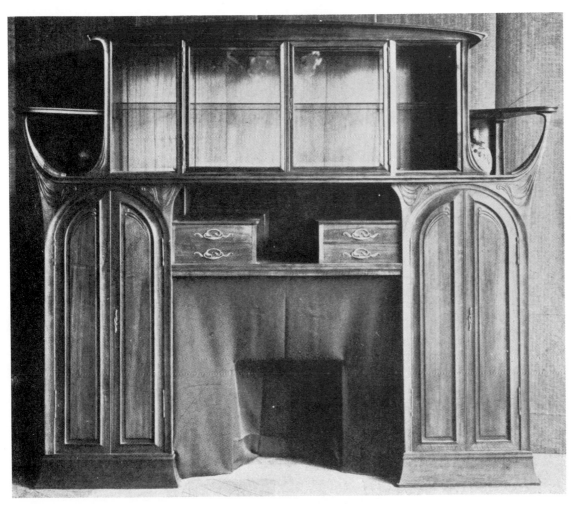

481

480. Desk, Henri Sauvage.   481. Fireplace and cabinet, Charles Plumet and Tony Selmersheim.

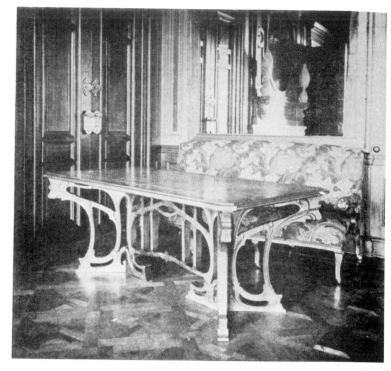

483

482

484

482. Chair, Louis Félix Bigaux.   483. Table, Victor Horta.   484. Bureau, Théodore Lambert.

485

486

485. Chair, Eugène Gaillard. 486. Table, Arno Max Robert Hérold.

487

487. *Armoire, Eugène Gaillard.*

488

488. *Buffet, Charles Albert Gautier.*

489

490

491

489. Corner table, Georges de Feure.   490 &491. Armoire and tea table, Henri Sauvage.

492

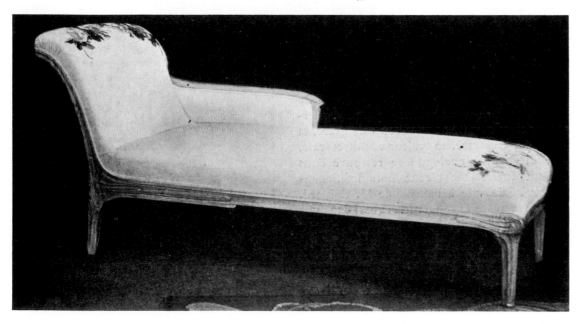

493

492. *Bookcase, Henri-Jules Ferdinand Bellery-Desfontaines.   493. Chaise longue, Georges de Feure.*

494

494. *Buffet, Louis Sorel.*

495

495. *Bookcase, Georges de Feure.*

496

497

496. *Serving table, Charles Plumet and Tony Selmersheim.*   497. *Sofa, Henri-Jules Ferdinand Bellery-Desfontaines.*

498

499

498. *Sofa, Charles Plumet and Tony Selmersheim.*   499. *Tea table, Louis Majorelle.*

500

500. *Buffet, Tony Selmersheim.*

501

501. *Bookcase, Louis Majorelle.*

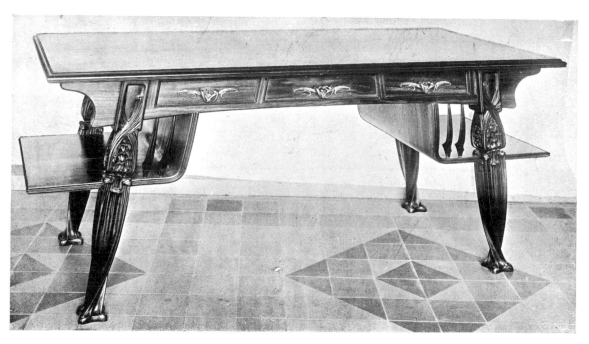

502

503

502. *Desk, Louis Majorelle.*   503. *Buffet, Mathieu Gallerey.*

504

505

504. *Etagère, Eugène Gaillard.*   505. *Buffet, Henri-Jules Ferdinand Bellery-Desfontaines.*

506

507

506. *Armchair, Edward Colonna.*   507. *Dresser, Louis Majorelle.*

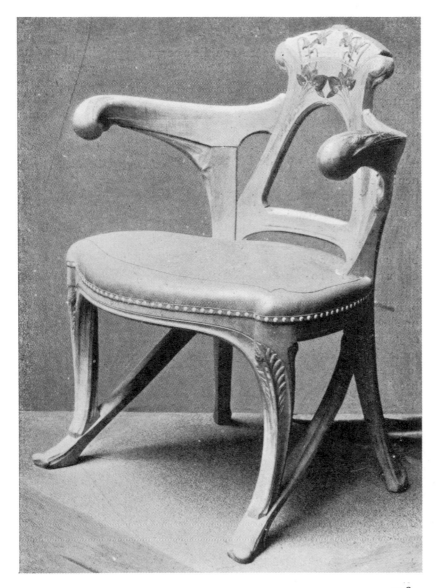

508

508. *Chair, Jean-Auguste Dampt.*

509

510

510. *Buffet, Léon Jallot.*

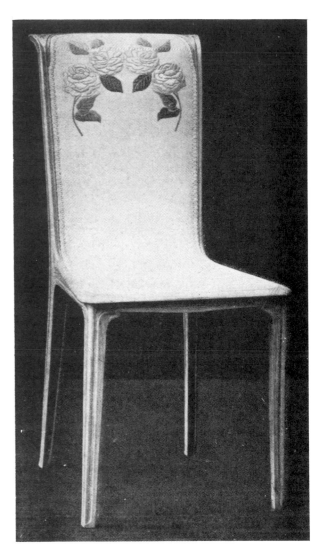

511

512

511. Dining-room cabinet, Louis Majorelle.   512. Chair, Georges de Feure.

513   514

513. *Table, Gustave Serrurier-Bovy.*   514. *Chair, Eugène Gaillard.*

515

515. *Buffet, Léon Jallot.*

516

516. Buffet, Paul Follot.

517

518

517. Bed and night table, Louis Majorelle.   518. Bed, Henri Sauvage.

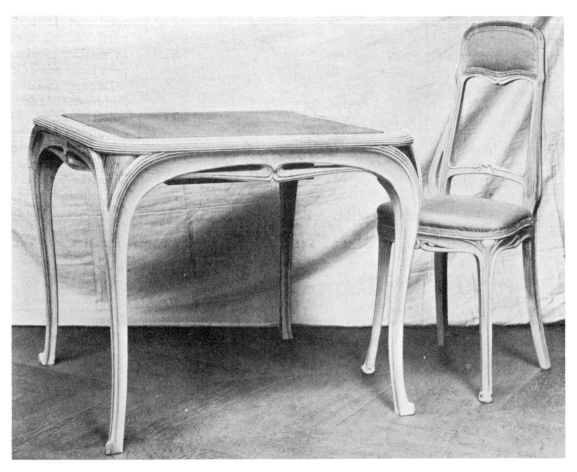

519

520

519. *Game table, Henri Sauvage.*   520. *Table, Edward Colonna.*

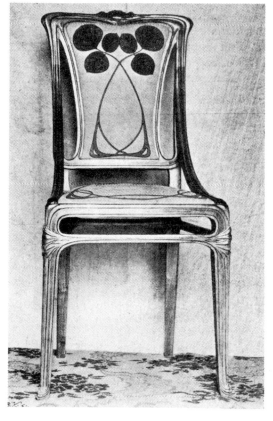

521

522

521. *Chair, Abel Landry.*   522. *Cabinet, Charles Plumet and Tony Selmersheim.*

523

524

523. *Cabinet, Emile Gallé.* 524. *Chair, Edward Colonna.*

525

525. *Buffet, Charles Plumet and Tony Selmersheim.*

526

526. *Buffet, Eugène Gaillard.*

527

528

527. *Bed, Henri-Jules Ferdinand Bellery-Desfontaines.*   528. *Commode, Louis Majorelle.*

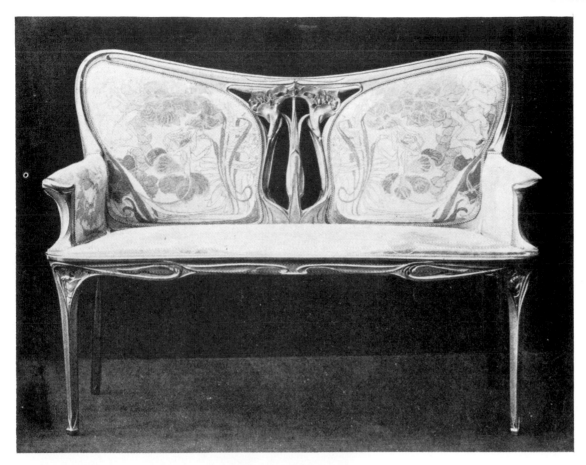

529

530

529 & 530. Sofa and bookcase, Georges de Feure.

531

532

531. Chair, Eugène Gaillard.   532. Buffet, Louis Sorel.

533

534

533. *Secretary, Hans Eduard von Berlepsch-Valendas.*   534. *Chair, Georges de Feure.*

535

535. *Bookcase, Pierre Selmersheim.*

536

536. *Screen, Georges de Feure.*

537

538

537. *Chair, Louis Majorelle.*   538. *Desk, Henri-Jules Ferdinand Bellery-Desfontaines.*

539

540

539. Etagère, Charles Plumet.   540. Chair, Eugène Gaillard.

541. Batik screen, Gerrit Willem Dijsselhof.

MISCELLANEOUS MATERIALS

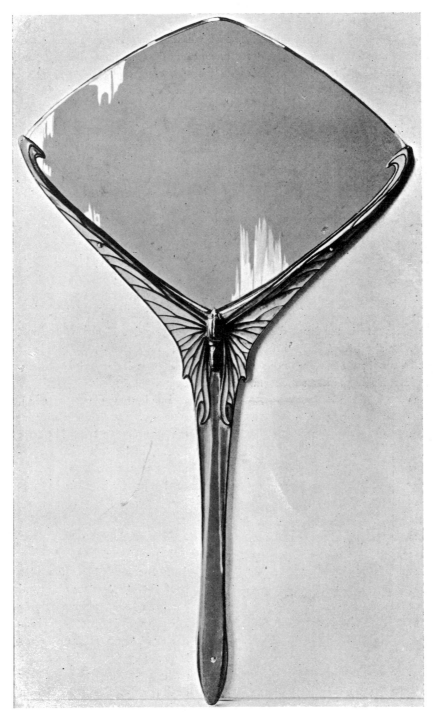

542. Mirror, René Lalique.

543

544

543. Doors, Jean-Auguste Dampt.   544. Letter opener, René Lalique.

545

546

547

545. *Bookbinding, Victor Prouvé.* 546 & 547. *Bookbindings, René Wiener.*

548

549

550

548. Door, Hans Eduard von Berlepsch-Valendas.   549. Bookbinding, Marius-Michel.   550. Buckle, Henri Hamm.

551

552

553

551. *Bookbinding, P. Claessens.*   552. *Mirror, Maurice Giot.*   553. *Bookbindings, Jessie M. King.*

554

555

556

554. *Clock, Maurice Dufrène.*   555. *Letter opener, Mathurin Méheut.*   556. *Handbag, Louise Germain.*

557

558

559

557. *Frieze, Charles Francis Annesley Voysey.*   558. *Bookbinding, Petrus Ruban.*   559. *Door, Louis Marnez and Léon Julien Ernest Sonnier.*

560

561

560. *Bookbinding, Charles Meunier.*   561. *Doors, G. & M. Soulié.*

562

563

562. *Bookbinding, Marius-Michel.* 563. *Letter opener, René Lalique.*

564

565

564. *Clock, Edmond Henri Becker.*   565. *Clock, Alexandre Charpentier and Tony Selmersheim.*

567

566

568

566. *Door, Hans Eduard von Berlepsch-Valendas.*   567. *Bookbinding, Léon Gruel.*   568. *Bookbinding, Victor Prouvé.*

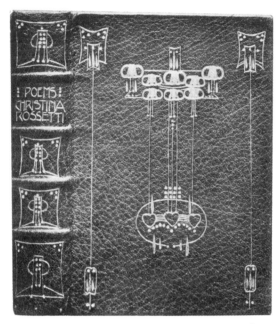

569

570

569. *Bookbinding, Jessie M. King.*   570. *Handbags, Mlle de Félice.*

572

573

571

571. Letter opener, René Lalique.   572. Bookbinding, Charles Meunier.   573. Letter holder, Edmond Henri Becker.

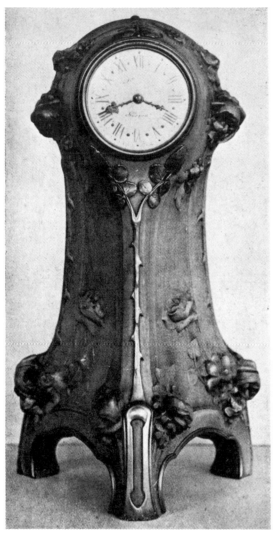

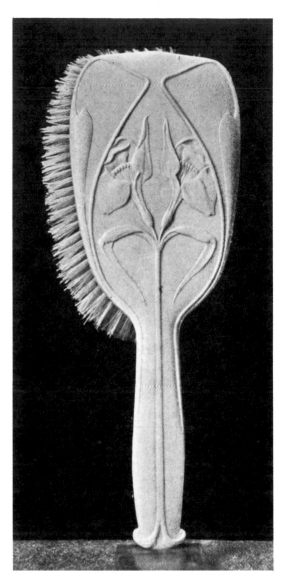

574

575

574. *Clock, Edmond Henri Becker.*   575. *Ivory hair brush, L'Art Nouveau Bing.*

576

577

578

576. *Lacquer and mother-of-pearl plaque, Lucien Gaillard.* 577 & 578. *Letter openers, René Lalique.*

579

579. *Three views of a clock, Edmond Henri Becker.*

BIOGRAPHICAL SKETCHES

ANDRÉ, EMILE (French: 1871–1933). The leading architect of the Nancy School. He also designed furniture. During the 1890's his Art Nouveau designs reflected the rococo tradition which had thrived in Nancy. After the turn of the century he developed a simpler, more austere style.

ANGST, CHARLES ALBERT (Swiss: b. 1875). Sculptor and artist-craftsman.

L'ART NOUVEAU BING. Applied art commissioned by Samuel Bing. His Parisian shop sold art objects and household furnishings executed in the "new style." The name of the shop eventually became accepted as the designation for the new art movement itself.

ASHBEE, CHARLES ROBERT (English: 1863–1942). Important figure in the English Arts and Crafts Movement. He founded the Guild and School of Handicraft in London in 1888.

BAILLIE-SCOTT, MACKAY HUGH (English: 1865–1945). Architect and interior designer. His decorations for the home of the Grand Duke of Hesse at Darmstadt made him the principal disseminator of the English arts-and-crafts style in Germany.

BARBOTEAU (French). Designer of bronze vases.

BAUMANN, LUDWIG (Austrian: 1853–1936). Viennese interior and industrial designer.

BECKER, EDMOND HENRI (French: b. 1871). Craftsman, woodcarver, and medalist. He collaborated with the Parisian jewelry firm Boucheron.

BEETZ-CHARPENTIER, ELISA (French). Dutch-born sculptor. Her work included statues, portraits of infants, dancers, and medals. She was a pupil of and later married Alexandre Charpentier.

BEHRENS, PETER (German: 1868–1940). Architect, illustrator, and artist-craftsman. He began his career as a painter. During the 1890's he was primarily a graphic artist and decorator. In 1893 he was one of the founders of the Munich Secession, from 1889–1903, a member of the artists' colony of Mathildehohe in Darmstadt; from 1903–1907, the head of the Dusseldorf Kunstgewerbeschule. In later years he taught architecture at Vienna and Berlin.

BELLERY-DESFONTAINES, HENRI-JULES FERDINAND (French: 1867–1910). Painter, craftsman, lithographer, and illustrator.

BELVILLE, EUGÈNE (French: 1863–1931). Artist-craftsman in leather and metal.

BENOUVILLE, LOUIS. No information available.

BERLEPSCH-VALENDAS, HANS EDUARD VON (Swiss: 1849–1921). Architect, painter, craftsman. He was influenced by Morris and the English Arts and Crafts Movement. He designed not only buildings and furniture, but also book bindings.

BESNARD, PAUL ALBERT (French: 1849–1934). Painter and printmaker. He studied at the École des Beaux-Arts and with Cabanal.

BIAIS, MAURICE (French). Decorator and illustrator.

BIGAUX, LOUIS FÉLIX (French). Painter and decorator, designer of tapestries and wallpaper. He organized a group of young artist-craftsmen to design all forms of fine and decorative arts.

BINET, RENÉ (French: 1866–1911). Architect and painter. He designed the main entrance of the Paris World's Fair of 1900.

BING AND GROENDHAL. Danish porcelain firm founded in 1853. The firm first won popular attention at the Paris Exhibition of 1900. They also designed glassware in the Japanese style.

BONVALLET, LUCIEN (French: *b.* 1861). Artist-craftsman. He designed models for Maison Cardeilhac in Paris and Sèvres. After 1885 he specialized in metalwork, creating mountings for work by Dalpayrat and Gallé.

BOTTÉE, LOUIS ALEXANDRE (French: 1852–1941). Sculptor and engraver of medals.

BOUCHERON, FRÉDÉRIC (French: 1830–1902). Founded his own successful jewelry firm in 1858. Among his clients were Americans who had seen the work of his designers at the Philadelphia Exhibition. Artists employed by his firm included Edmond Becker and Jules Debut. After his death in 1902 his son Louis managed the firm.

BRANDT, EDGAR W. (French: *b.* 1880). Metalwork designer.

BRANDT, PAUL-EMILE (Swiss). Jewelry designer.

BRANGWYN, FRANK (English: 1867–1943). Painter, printmaker, and craftsman. He studied at South Kensington Art School and served an apprenticeship in William Morris's workshop. He designed furniture, textiles, and carpets.

BRINDEAU DE JARNY, PAUL (French). Artist-craftsman. His work appeared in the decorative art section of the Salon d'Automne from 1909–1930.

BRÉANT AND COULBAUX. No information available.

BRUCKMANN. German silverware firm, founded in the eighteenth century by George Peter Bruckmann and operated in the late nineteenth century by Peter and Ernst B. Bruckmann.

BUGATTI, CARLO (Italian: *b.* ca. 1855). Interior designer and decorator. He was best known for his furniture made of parchment.

CHAPLET, ERNEST (French: 1835–1909). Potter known for his stoneware and porcelain. He worked at Sèvres and later managed the Haviland factory. After 1884 he produced ceramics under his own name and developed the artistic possibilities of decorative glazes. In 1886 he collaborated with Gauguin.

CHARPENTIER, ALEXANDRE (French: 1856–1909). Sculptor. He was also known as a graphic artist and designer of furniture, metal, ceramic and leather objects. He was a member of "Les Cinq," later called "Les Six" and "L'Art dans Tout," a French arts and crafts association.

CHEDANNE, GEORGES (French: 1861–1940). Architect. He practiced primarily in Paris.

CLAESSENS, P. No information available.

COLONNA, EDWARD [EUGÈNE] (French: 1862–1948). Decorative artist, interior and furniture designer. He was active in the firm L'Art Nouveau. His work includes designs for jewelry, pottery, textiles, and glass. He made several trips to the United States and worked briefly with Associated Artists in New York.

COUDYSER, JULES (French). Artist-decorator. He specialized in designs for embroidery and lace.

COUTY, EDME (French: *d.* 1917). Painter and decorator. He designed tapestries, furniture, and book covers and worked for the Sèvres porcelain factory.

DALPAYRAT, ADRIEN PIERRE (French: 1844–1910). Potter. His firm specialized in glaze effects on stoneware and porcelain. He collaborated with Adèle Lesbros and Voisin Delacroix to manufacture stoneware at reasonable prices. He worked for Meier-Graefe at La Maison Moderne. His own pieces were mounted occasionally by Cardeilhac.

DAMMOUSE, ALBERT-LOUIS (French: 1848–1926). Son of a sculptor at the Sèvres porcelain factory. He studied sculpture and experimented with the decoration of porcelain. While he worked at Sèvres, he was particularly interested in glaze effects on porcelain and stoneware. He later experimented with glass.

DAMPT, JEAN-AUGUSTE (French: 1853–1946). Sculptor, engraver and craftsman. He was best known for his light fixtures inspired by plant forms.

D'ARONCO, RAIMONDO (Italian: 1857–1932). Architect. His work was influenced by the seventeenth-century architect Guarino Guarini, the style of Charles Rennie Mackintosh, and the Vienna Secession. He designed buildings in Italy and Turkey.

DAVIDSON, PETER WYLER (English: *d.* 1933). Jewelry designer.

DECOEUR, EMILE (French: 1876–1953). Potter. He was first apprenticed to and later collaborated with Edmond Lachenal. At first studied faience, glazes, and firing techniques. Later he gave up faience for stoneware.

DELAHERCHE, AUGUSTE (French: 1857–1940). One of the most important French Art Nouveau potters. He bought and operated Ernest Chaplet's workshop from 1887 to 1894 and was associated periodically with Samuel Bing. After 1904 he made only unique pieces, usually stoneware. Like many of his contemporaries he admired Japanese and Chinese earthenware.

DERAISME, GEORGES PIERRE (French: b. 1865). Sculptor. He was a member of the Societé Centrale des Arts Décoratifs.

DIJSSELHOF, GERRIT WILLEM (Dutch: 1866–1924). Painter and leader in the Dutch decorative-arts movement. His textiles were influenced by batik designs from Java, his furniture by the English Arts and Crafts Movement.

DUFAT, F. No information available.

DUFRÈNE, MAURICE (French: 1876–1925). Designer of furniture, rugs, jewelry, wallpaper, and bookbindings. He studied at the Ecole des Arts Décoratifs and after 1899 was a craftsman for La Maison Moderne. He later renounced Art Nouveau and became a spokesman for industrial techniques.

DULONG, E. A. R. (French: b. 1860). Architect. He designed the principal restaurant at the Paris World's Fair of 1900.

DUNAND, JEAN (Swiss: 1877–1942). Sculptor and craftsman in metal. He studied sculpture with Jean Dampt. After the turn of the century he experimented with beaten metal. His first metal vases were in the Art Nouveau style, though later he renounced organic forms for more geometric shapes.

ECKMANN, OTTO (German: 1865–1902). Munich graphic artist and designer. He gave up painting in 1894 to devote his time to the decorative arts. His interest in nature and Japanese art are reflected in his ornaments for the German periodicals *Pan* and *Jugend.* He also designed furniture, stained glass, wallpaper, textiles, and rugs.

FALKE, GISELA DE (Austrian). Viennese artist-craftsman in glass, ceramics, and metal. She studied with Joseph Hoffmann.

FARMAKOWSKY (Russian: b. 1873). Studied in Russia, Germany, and finally Paris.

FÉLICE, MLLE DE. No information available.

FEUILLÂTRE, EUGÈNE (French: 1870–1916). Sculptor, goldsmith, and craftsman in enamel. He first worked for René Lalique and later established his own workshop.

FEURE, GEORGES DE (French: 1868–1928). Painter, printmaker, artist-craftsman. Designer of furniture, tapestries, porcelain, stoneware, book ornament, and posters. Samuel Bing commissioned several interior designs for his shop L'Art Nouveau, as well as furnishings for his pavillion at the World's Fair in 1900.

FINCH, ALFRED WILLIAM (Belgian: 1854–1930). Painter, ceramist, and printmaker. He visited England in 1866 and introduced the English Arts and Crafts Movement to Henry van der Velde and "Les Vingt." Later he was the head of a ceramic workshop and a school for crafts in Finland.

FISHER, ALEXANDER (English: 1864–1936). Painter and craftsman. His interest in Celtic art was reflected in his work as a goldsmith. He popularized enamel crafts in England.

FLEURET. No information available.

FOLLOT, PAUL (French: 1877–1911). Decorator. A pupil of Eugène Grasset, his designs include furniture and table settings. He worked for Samuel Bing at L'Art Nouveau and for Meier-Graefe at La Maison Moderne.

FOUQUET, GEORGES (French: 1862–1957). He operated a jewelry firm established by his father in 1860. He collaborated with designers such as Desrosiers and Mucha.

GAILLARD, EUGÈNE (French: 1862–1933). Architect and furniture designer. His work for Samuel Bing included the pavillion at the Paris World's Fair of 1900, along with Edward Colonna and Georges de Feure.

GAILLARD, LUCIEN (French: b. 1861). Jeweler and operator of the family firm. He drew his artistic inspiration from nature—plants, flowers, animals, and insects—and from Japanese art.

GALLÉ, EMILE (French: 1846–1904). Leader of the Nancy School of Art Nouveau. He was a versatile craftsman who designed furniture, pottery, and glassware. Although his early work borrowed heavily from historical prototypes, his interest in botany was soon reflected in the naturalistic motifs found in his designs, which often included literary inscriptions. The Gallé glassworks continued until the 1930's.

GALLEREY, MATHIEU. No information available.

GARDEY, L. No information available.

GARNIER, ANTOINE (TONY) (French: 1869–1948). Painter and architect. He is best known for his revolutionary plans for an "Industrial City" (1901–1904).

GAUDIN, FÉLIX (French). Designer of stained glass.

GAUTIER, CHARLES ALBERT (French: b. 1846). Painter and architect.

GÉRARD, E. No information available.

GERMAIN, LOUISE (French: b. 1880). Painter in watercolors and artist-craftsman. She specialized in leatherwork and designed book covers.

GESELLIUS, HERMAN (Finnish: 1876–1916). Architect. From 1897–1904 he was associated with Armas Lindgren and Eliel Saarinen.

GINZKEY. No information available.

GIOT, MAURICE (French). Landscape painter, decorator, and lithographer.

GLASGOW SCHOOL OF ART. School of fine and decorative art which became associated with the Art Nouveau movement in Scotland. The leader of this national style was Charles Rennie Mackintosh, who was assisted by his wife Margaret Macdonald, her sister Frances Macdonald, and her husband Herbert MacNair. "The Four" and their followers produced household items from furniture to embroidery, metalwork and book illustration.

GLATIGNY. French atelier, established in the 1890's, which produced porcelain.

GOLDSMITHS AND SILVERSMITHS CO., LTD. British firm that produced household objects in gold and silver. It was established early in the 1890's.

GRASSET, EUGÈNE (French: 1841–1917). Trained as an architect. As a decorator and illustrator, his designs were influenced by Japanese and Celtic art. As an art theorist and a naturalist, he published books on design and ornament. He designed mosaics, ceramics, stained glass windows, and jewelry.

GRUBER, JACQUES (French: b. 1870). Painter and craftsman. He designed furniture and jewelry in Paris and Nancy.

GRUEBY. American pottery firm established by William H. Grueby in 1894. By the end of the century the firm had developed a characteristic style—vases with heavy shapes decorated with either floral or severe geometric designs. Grueby architectural tiles were popular throughout the country.

GRUEL, LÉON (French). Bookbinder. He often used stylized plant shapes as decoration.

GUFFROY, MME. No information available.

GUIMARD, HECTOR (French: 1867–1942). Architect and sculptor. He was one of the most successful French Art Nouveau designers. He was influenced by English domestic architecture, the work of Victor Horta in Belgium, and by his study of nature. He used cast iron extensively in his buildings which include the entrances to the Paris Métro, the Ecole du Sacré-Coeur, Castel Béranger, Castel Henriette in Sèvres, and the Humbert de Romans building. He designed the interiors as well, from the floors to the lighting fixtures.

HABERT-DYS, JULES AUGUSTE (French: b. 1850). Painter and engraver. He made designs for Sèvres porcelain.

HAMM, HENRI (French: b. 1871). Artist-craftsman and decorator.

HANKAR, PAUL (Belgium: 1859–1901). Architect and furniture designer. His constructive and rectilinear style was influenced by Oriental art and the English Arts and Crafts Movement.

HANSEN-JACOBSEN, NIELS (Danish: b. 1861). Sculptor and ceramist.

HARVEY, AGNES BANKIER (British). Designer of metal and enamel jewelry. She was a member of the Glasgow School of Art.

HÉROLD, ARNO MAX ROBERT (German: b. 1871). Architect.

HOENTSCHEL, GEORGES (French: 1855–1915). Architect, sculptor, ceramist. He drew inspiration for his designs from nature and Japanese art, with little attempt at stylization.

HOFFMANN, JOSEF (Austrian: 1870–1956). Architect, illustrator, and designer. He studied architecture with Otto Wagner in Vienna, provided illustrations for the Art Nouveau journal *Ver Sacrum*, and was one of the founders of the Vienna Secession. Later he was a professor of architecture at the Wiener Kunstgewerbeschule and with Koloman Moser he established the Vienna Werkstätte in 1903. A hallmark of his work was the square or checkerboard pattern.

HOHLWEIN, LUDWIG (German: 1874–1949). Architect, painter, craftsman. He designed furnishings, ceramics, posters, and books.

HORTA, VICTOR (Belgian: 1861–1947). Architect. He trained in Paris and Brussels and inherited Alphonse Balat's architectural firm. He introduced a mature Art Nouveau style to Brussels in 1892, using exposed metal structure, glass, and ornament to fuse his architectural designs and interior decoration into a cohesive whole.

HOUSTON, MARY GALWAY (British: b. 1871). Artist-craftsman. She wrote many books on historical costumes and decoration.

HUSSON, HENRI (French: 1852–1914). Goldsmith and designer of jewelry and silverware.

JALLOT, LÉON (French: active c. 1895–1910). Furniture designer. He worked for Samuel Bing.

KING, JESSIE M. (Scottish). Illustrator and bookbinder. She trained at the Glasgow Art School.

KOEPPING, KARL (German: 1848–1914). Painter, printmaker, craftsman in glass.

KRASNIK, MLLE. Viennese painter and craftsman. A pupil of Koloman Moser at the Kunstgewerbeschule, she did portraits of women and children.

LÄUGER, MAX (German: 1864–1952). Architect, teacher, and artist-potter. He specialized in simple and traditional Oriental vase shapes and later ran a workshop that made majolica for the Majolika-Manufaktur in Karlsruhe.

LAFFITTE, G. (French). Jewelry designer.

LAFFITTE AND WASLEY. No information available on Wasley. See G. Laffitte.

LALIQUE, RENÉ JULES (French: 1860–1945). Jewelry designer. He served an apprenticeship with the goldsmith Louis Aucoc and had his own workshop in Paris in 1885 where he worked in gold, silver and enamel. After 1900 he began working in glass. His designs were particularly popular in the 1920's.

LAMBERT, THÉODORE (French: b. 1857). Architect and artist-craftsman. He designed jewelry and home furnishings, including furniture and lighting fixtures.

LANDRY, ABEL (French). Trained as a landscape painter and as an architect. He concentrated on interior design after he studied with William Morris, the English artist-craftsman. He designed interiors for the Paris firm La Maison Moderne. He preferred to create complete interiors, including wallpaper and curtains.

LAPORTE-BLAIRSY, LÉO (French: 1865–1922). Sculptor, printmaker, and craftsman. He specialized in lighting fixtures.

LEBEAU, JORIS JOHANNES CHRISTIAAN (Dutch: 1876–1946). Printmaker, poster artist, and craftsman. He designed textiles and glass.

LEBÈGUE, LÉON (French). Painter and illustrator.

LELIÈVRE, EUGÈNE (French: b. 1856). Sculptor. He was one of the founding members of the Artistes Décorateurs.

LEVEILLÉ, ERNEST MICHEL (French). Operated a firm that produced glass and porcelain. In 1885 he acquired Rousseau's glassworks and continued the Japanesque style of that house.

LHUER, VICTOR (French). Artist-craftsman. He designed fabrics and wrote several books on costumes.

LIBERTY & CO. English furnishers and drapers' shop established by Arthur Lasenby Liberty in 1875. A principal disseminator of Art Nouveau articles in England, Liberty often commissioned his own designs to be offered in the store. This association with Art Nouveau designs gave the style one of its many names—Stile Liberty.

LIÉNARD, PAUL (French: 1849–1900). Sculptor, artist-craftsman, and jewelry designer.

LINDGREN, ARMAS (1874–1929). Architect. From 1897–1904 he was associated with Herman Gesellius and Eliel Saarinen.

MACBETH, ANN (Scottish). Scottish artist-craftsman. She designed and executed embroidery.

MACDONALD, FRANCES (Scottish: 1874–1921). Artist-craftsman and designer. One of the Glasgow "Four," she taught enameling and metalwork at the Glasgow School of Art. She married Herbert Mac-Nair, also a member of the "Four."

MACDONALD, MARGARET (Scottish: 1865–1933). Artist-craftsman and designer. One of the Glasgow "Four," she married C. R. Mackintosh. She worked in metal and stained glass and later decorated gesso panels.

MACKINTOSH, CHARLES RENNIE (Scottish: 1868–1928). Major British architect of the 1880's. He was also an interior designer and leader of the Glasgow "Four." His work includes furniture, light fixtures, and household decoration, along with the Glasgow School of Art, Windyhill (a private home), and the Scottish pavilion at the Turin Exposition.

MacNair, Frances M. (see Macdonald, Frances).

MacNair, Herbert (Scottish: *b.* 1870). Architect and artist-craftsman, one of the Glasgow "Four."

Maison Cardeilhac. French silversmith firm. Established in 1804, it first made flatware and cutlery. Ernest Cardeilhac (1851–1904) expanded the firm to include gold and silversmithing.

La Maison Moderne. Parisian shop specializing in Art Nouveau objects. Founded in 1897 by the German art critique Meier-Graefe, it sold the works of Maurice Dufrène, Henry van de Velde, and others.

Maison Vever. French jewelry firm established by Ernest Vever. He retired in 1880 and was succeeded by his sons Paul (1851–1915) and Henri (1854–1942). Their jewelry was usually based on motifs from nature. Henri created some designs himself, along with Edward Colonna and Eugène Grasset.

Majorelle, Louis (French: 1859–1926). Artist-craftsman. He was closely associated with Emile Gallé at Nancy where he operated his father's furniture and ceramics factory. His plastic Art Nouveau designs suggest Rococo influence.

Marnez, Louis (French). Architect.

Martin, Henri (French: *b.* 1860). Neo-impressionist painter. He also decorated interiors.

Méheut, Mathurin (French: 1882–1958). Painter, draftsman, wood engraver, book illustrator, ceramist, and designer of tapestry and lace.

Meier, Emil (Austrian: *b.* 1877). Viennese sculptor and ceramic artist.

Meissen. German porcelain firm established in 1710.

Meunier, Charles (French: *b.* 1866). Parisian writer and bookbinder.

Michel, Henri François (also known as Marius-Michel) (French: 1846–1927). Bookbinder. He established an atelier with his father in 1876. His designs were often based on floral motifs.

Moreau-Nélaton, Etienne (French: 1859–1927). Painter, ceramist, writer on art. He was a collector of nineteenth-century French painting and a member of the French crafts society, "Les Cinq."

Morice, Mlle. No information available.

Morisset, Mlle. No information available.

Moser, Koloman (Austrian: 1868–1918). Painter, printmaker, craftsman, and teacher. He encouraged the Austrian Arts and Crafts Movement, especially book and poster design, through his work, his writings, and teaching. He was one of the founders of the Vienna Secession in 1897. In 1903 he established the Vienna Werkstätte with Hoffmann and Warndorfer.

Mucha, Alphonse (French, born Moravia, 1860–1933). Printmaker and illustrator. He is best known for his posters publicizing Sarah Bernhardt. He also made designs for applied art, including jewelry, textiles, and furniture.

Ory-Robin, Mme. No information available.

Paul, Bruno (German: *b.* 1874). Painter, printmaker, and decorative artist. He did illustrations for the German magazine, *Jugend.* In 1897 he founded the Vereinigte Werkstätten für Kunst in Munich with Bernhard Pankok. Later (1924–1932) he was the director of the Vereinigte Staatsschule für freie und angewandte Kunst in Berlin.

Plumet, Charles (French: 1861–1928). Architect, craftsman, and calligrapher. His interior designs and furniture were often made in collaboration with Tony Selmersheim. He was the architect-in-chief of the Paris World's Fair of 1900.

James Powell and Sons. English glassmaking firm. Its association with the Arts and Crafts Movement was established when William Morris commissioned the company to manufacture a table glass designed by Philip Webb. After 1880 the firm was run by Harry J. Powell, who remained in control until World War I.

Pradelle, Georges (French: *b.* 1865). Architect.

Prévot, Gabriel (French). Designer of lace and embroidery.

Prouvé, Victor Emile (French: 1858–1943). Sculptor, painter, medalist, printmaker, and artist-craftsman. He studied and worked with Emile Gallé and Louis Majorelle. He provided designs for book bindings, glassware, ceramics, jewelry, embroidery, lace, and marquetry decoration. Later he was director of the Ecole des Beaux Arts in Nancy.

Ranson, Paul Elie (French: 1862–1909). Painter, printmaker, and artist-craftsman. He designed ceramics and tapestries. He was one of the founders of the French group of decorative artists, the "Nabis," whose membership included Maurice Denis, Pierre Bonnard and Edouard Vuillard.

RAPIN, HENRI (French: *b.* 1873). Painter and decorator.

RATHBONE, RICHARD LLEWELYN BENSON (English). Designer of jewelry.

REGIUS. No information available.

GEORGES DE RIBAUCOURT (French: 1881–1907). Sculptor, decorator, and jewelry designer. He trained as an industrial artist.

RIVAUD, CHARLES (French: 1859–1923). Decorator and designer of metal jewelry.

RIVIÈRE, MME P. No information available.

ROBERT, EMILE (French: 1860–1924). Designer of ironwork. He first exhibted at the Union Centrale des Arts Décoratifs.

ROOKWOOD. American pottery firm, established in 1880 by Maria Longworth Nichols Stoter in Cincinnati, Ohio. The pottery of this company reflects a strong Oriental influence, introduced in part by the Japanese exhibit at the Philadelphia World's Fair of 1876. One of the potters who worked for the firm was Japanese.

ROUSSEAU, EUGÈNE (French: 1827–1891). Designer and artist-craftsman. He first designed ceramics and later produced glassware. Along with Emile Gallé, he was one of the most influential craftsmen working in the Japanese style. He is best known for his cased glass in which designs are engraved on a colorful outer layer to reveal a translucent inner layer of glass.

ROYAL COPENHAGEN. Danish factory established in 1722 to produce Delft ware. At the end of the nineteenth century, the firm produced "Aluminia" faience, decorated by stencil color-spraying. During this period Japanese influence was strong.

ROZENBURG. Dutch ceramic firm established during the last quarter of the nineteenth century. T. A. C. Colenbrander guided the manufactory during much of the 1880's. Later J. Juriaan Kok introduced his own Art Nouveau style.

RUBAN, PETRUS (French: *b.* 1851). Bookbinder.

RUBINSTEIN, ARTHUR (Austrian: *b.* 1873). Artist and craftsman.

SAARINEN, ELIEL (Finnish: 1873–1950). Leading architect of Finland until 1920 when he came to the United States. As a student he had studied painting and later designed interior furnishings. At the turn of the century he worked in partnership with Herman Gesellius and A. E. Lindgren.

SABON, MME MARTIN. No information available.

SAUVAGE, HENRI (French: 1873–1932). Architect, painter, and sculptor. He was one of the members of the informal French crafts association, "L'Art dans Tout," which included Charpentier, Dampt, Aubert, Moreau-Nélaton, Plumet, and Nocq.

SCHEIDECKER, PAUL FRANK (French, born in England). Painter, craftsman, and designer of silverware.

SCHMIDT-PECHT, ELISABETH. Artist-potter.

SCHMUZ-BAUDISZ, THEODOR HERMANN (German: 1859–1942). Painter and ceramist. From 1908–1926 he was director of the Staatliche Porzellan Manufaktur in Berlin.

SEGUIN, PIERRE (French: *b.* 1872). Sculptor and decorator. He studied and later taught at the Ecole Supérieure des Arts Décoratifs.

SEGUY, E. A. (French). Designer and artist. Several portfolios of his designs were printed in the pochoir process in Paris between 1900 and 1931.

SELMERSHEIM, PIERRE (French: *b.* 1869). Decorator and craftsman. He was the son of the architect Antoine Paul Selmersheim. He often collaborated with Charles Plumet, as did his brother Tony Selmersheim.

SELMERSHEIM, TONY (French: *b.* 1871). Artist-craftsman. He was a member of the French crafts association, "Les Cinq," later called "Les Six."

SERRURIER-BOVY, GUSTAVE (Belgian: 1858–1910). Interior designer and furniture maker. Trained as an architect, he devoted himself to the crafts movement after a trip to England, where he came under the influence of William Morris.

SÈVRES. French ceramics firm established in 1752. At the end of the nineteenth century the firm was divided into artistic and technical divisions. Its decoration reflects the contemporary Art Nouveau style.

SHERREBEK. Tapestry firm established by the pastor of Scheswig-Holstein-Jacobsen who decided to revive an old local industry of rug manufacture. A number of important artists designed for the firm, including Otto Eckmann and Hans Thoma.

SIKA, JUTTA (Austrian: 1877–1964). Painter and artist-craftsman. She studied with Moser and Roller at the Kunstgewerbeschule in Vienna. She was one of the founders of "Wiener Kunst im Hause" and designed ceramics, glass, and furniture for the firm Böck and the Wiener Werkstätte.

SIMPSON, EDGAR (English). No information available.

SOCARD, EDMOND (French: b. 1869). Painter of stained glass windows.

SONNIER, LÉON JULIEN ERNEST (French). Painter. He designed the decorations for Maxim's Restaurant in Paris in collaboration with the architect Louis Marnez.

SOREL, LOUIS (French: b. 1867). Swiss-born Parisian architect.

SOULIÉ, G. and M. No information available.

SPENCE, ISABEL (Scottish). Member of the Glasgow School of Art. No other information available.

STURBELLE, CAMILLE MARC (Belgian: b. 1873). Sculptor and craftsman. He designed a variety of objects, including vases, mirrors and clocks.

SZABO, A. G. (Hungarian). Designer of metalwork. He worked in Paris.

THORN-PRIKKER, JOHAN (Dutch: 1868–1932). Furniture and textile designer. His work was influenced by batik patterns from Java.

TIFFANY, LOUIS COMFORT (American: 1848–1933). Painter who later became interested in the decorative arts. He established Associated Artists, a firm which specialized in interior decoration in the early 1880's, and in 1885 the Tiffany Glass Company, which produced stained glass windows. In the 1890's his firm created "Favrille" glass, along with lamps, jewelry, furniture, and textiles.

VALLIN, EUGÈNE (French: 1856–1925). Furniture designer. His work is closely associated with Louis Majorelle, a fellow member of the Nancy school.

VAL-SAINT-LAMBERT. Belgian firm that produced glassware, established in the early nineteenth century. Not until after 1900 did the designs reflect the contemporary Art Nouveau style. Artists who provided designs included Henry van der Velde, Philippe Wolfers, and Gustave Serrurier-Bovy.

VELDE, HENRY VAN DE (Belgian: 1863–1957). Painter, artist-craftsman, architect and theoretician. He designed his own house in 1895 and produced a wide variety of crafts, including porcelain and stoneware, as well as furniture. In 1906, on the invitation of the Grand Duke of Saxe-Weimar, he became the head of the Weimar School for Arts and Crafts until World War I. He was instrumental in the founding of the Deutscher Werkbund in 1907.

VERNEUIL, MAURICE PILLARD (French: b. 1869). Poster artist and craftsman. He wrote a study on design in flowers and plants.

VEVER, HENRI (French: 1854–1942). Designer of jewelry. With his brother Paul he operated the firm Maison Vever, founded by their father Ernest Vever. They took part in the French Exhibitions of 1878 and 1889, though the real fame of the firm was not established until 1900. They and René Lalique were the leaders of French jewelry design. Edward Colonna and Eugène Grasset also worked for Maison Vever.

VLECK, KARL. No information available.

VOYSEY, CHARLES FRANCIS ANNESLEY (English: 1857–1941). Architect. He specialized in the design of the small country house. As a craftsman he designed furniture, carpets, wallpaper, and household utensils. He was one of the important spokesmen for the English Arts and Crafts Movement.

WALTON, GEORGE (English: 1867–1939). Architect and interior designer. He trained at the Glasgow School of Art.

WIENER, RENÉ (French: 1856–1939). Decorator and bookbinder.

WOLFERS, PHILIPPE (Belgian: 1858–1929). Jeweler. He first joined the family firm, Wolfers Frères, the Belgian crown jewelers, and later established his own workshop. During the 1890's he used ivory extensively in his designs, which were based on natural forms—plants, animals, the human figure. After 1905 he gradually abandoned jewelry and interior design for sculpture.

INDEX OF ARTISTS

The references are to figure numbers.